Choose Better

Choose Better

THE OPTIMAL DECISION-MAKING FRAMEWORK

Timothy Yen, Psy.D.

LIONCREST
PUBLISHING

CHOOSE BETTER
The Optimal Decision-Making Framework

ISBN   978-1-5445-1819-0   *Hardcover*
       978-1-5445-1818-3   *Paperback*
       978-1-5445-1817-6   *Ebook*

To my wife, the best decision I have ever made.

Contents

Introduction

"It's time. I'm filing for divorce." Meet Mary. I sat across the room from a woman who looked like an empty shell. She looked at me with a mixture of shock, disappointment, anger, and exhaustion. Mary has been in her marriage for the past 17 years and has three children with her husband. Her idea of marriage was "until death do us part," so she never imagined divorce would ever happen. For many years, she knew that there were problems in the marriage but she turned a blind eye. Mary did not deal with the problems due to her fear of making the wrong choice. She feared that her husband would become verbally abusive or hurt the kids if she voiced her concerns. What if she confronted him and her situation got worse? Mary was in a place of indecision about what to do and in the end, she suffered for it. She lived in fear and emptiness for years. Her children were negatively impacted by their unhealthy marriage. Why was she so indecisive? How would things be different if she had made the decision to speak up earlier?

Meet Joe, Mary's soon-to-be ex-husband. Joe sat in the chair across from Mary. His arms were crossed and he looked angry. Upon further discussion, his frustration was primarily with himself. After many years of building a family with Mary, he never planned on getting a divorce either. Mary was the love of his life! They were high school sweethearts and he wanted to grow old with her. Joe dreamed of getting a family cabin where his grandkids would make memories like when he was a boy. Those dreams died with this divorce. As much as he wanted to remain married, he made some awful choices. Joe had an alcohol problem. He would drink to numb his emotional pain. He admitted that he would often take his anger out on Mary and say venomous things. His kids were scared of him, and the police were called several times. His own father used to drink too much, and he hated when his father drank. Ironically, he was in the same place now as his father: losing the people he loved the most. Joe also saw the signs of his declining marriage and told himself: "I am going to stop drinking and make things right with my wife." That day never came. If he was honest with himself, he did not want to change. It was easier to drink and suppress. He made poor choices, which led to divorce. Why could he not make better choices? I've heard that divorce is the second most emotionally painful experience a person can have, the first being the death of your child. The majority of people do not pursue a marriage with divorce in mind. In fact, people are genuinely in love with one another, which is why they decide to commit for life. Sometimes, people get out of a marriage thinking that things will get better and the pain will stop. Unfortunately, the opposite is usually true. The pain gets exacerbated especially when courts gets involved and child custody becomes a bitter fight. People even begin contemplating suicide because the situation seems to drag on unendingly, and death starts to call out with the draw of promising peace. How does something like this happen? To put it simply, terrible outcomes result from a series of poor decisions.

Mary and Joe illustrate the two kinds of people this book is written for. They both have decision-making problems that led to the end of their most important relationship. Mary captures an individual who has the problem of indecision. She is paralyzed with fear or confusion when a challenge arises, and she chooses to do nothing. Mary is often seen as a nice person who avoids conflict at all cost. She lacks self-confidence and feels like her voice is insignificant. There are often strong feelings of sadness or resentment, but she has learned to suppress those feelings in fear that people will reject her if she speaks up. She tends to "go with the flow" but often feels dismissed as an individual. Her life feels disempowered, and she secretly admires those who seem so sure of themselves.

Joe embodies the individual who has the problem of making poor choices. He has no problem reacting to a situation but often does so in an impulsive kind of way. Joe tends to rush into a decision out of anxiety or frustration without really thinking things through. When he makes a bad decision, he does not admit it. He is quick to justify and rationalize his decisions, but he cannot deny how much he hates the consequences. Joe tends to blame other people or situations for his current outcomes but secretly hates himself for being the problem. He may appear to be confident and opinionated when making his decisions, but self-doubt is ever present when poor choices are made. Instead of learning from his mistakes, he chooses to ignore the problem and deceive himself into thinking it will never happen again...until it happens again. Same song, different tune. Joe creates a disappointing life and does not know how to live differently.

Who are you? Indecisive Mary or Poor Choice Joe? I will admit, I have been both. There are times when I have trouble making a decision. Other times, I get emotional and make poor choices. Maybe you are somewhere in between. I am sure you know people in your life like Mary and Joe. In both cases, they live less-than-optimal lives. Both Mary and Joe were acting in ways that were beneath their potential. At the very least, their lives did not reflect what they desired to create.

If you can see yourself in Mary or Joe, you are not alone. There are perfectly sensible reasons for the struggle. Every behavior has a function. This means that every decision we make benefits us in some way or else we stop doing those things. Some of you may have come from difficult childhoods, where your mother or father made bad decisions and you had to suffer because of them. Others may have been born with certain deficits or disabilities that made you feel different from those around you. There are certainly things that happen to us that are outside of our control and absolutely not our fault. We can easily rationalize our choices to disengage from trying and continue to make poor decisions that betray our true identity. Or you can resolve to change. This is an important choice you must make, and it begins now. You must make the resolution to take back your power to choose. Decision-making is your responsibility, not anyone else's. We must give up our position as victims of our circumstances.

I am calling forth greatness and a better destiny for your life. Despite all of the reasons why you have difficulties making decisions or continue to make bad ones, you can change! If I did not believe this to be true, I would quit being a psychologist. I have seen countless people turn their lives around because they learned how to think more clearly and make better decisions. They began experiencing authentic living and became their desired version of themselves. You, too, can experience greater mental clarity and identity that leads to strong self-esteem and genuine confidence. Optimal decision-making can fundamentally shift your perspective on life. It can help you experience yourself as an empowered game changer. It lets you know who you are, what you want, and how to get it.

I have the honor of being your guide to becoming your desired self. You will learn ways to gain a deeper understanding of why you get stuck and make poor decisions. Instead of figuring things out on the spot during moments of chaos, you will have a practical protocol that guides you to clarify the problem and identify the optimal choice. I call this protocol the Framework. The Framework process will help you get unstuck and will help you know what step to take next. We will also address the potential pitfalls of making poor choices and how you can summon the courage to implement your optimal choice.

Who am I and why should you trust me to be your guide? I am a clinical psychologist who has seen literally thousands of clients (both in the hospital and in private practice settings) who struggle with poor decision-making. My clients' indecision or poor decisions have largely contributed to their dissatisfying lives. I took the time to evaluate how people become better through counseling, and I developed the Framework to support people in their healing and identity formation. As an international speaker and seminar facilitator, I have witnessed leaders and teams across multiple cultures become empowered individuals who are able to live their best lives now.

Is this book for you? It depends. If you are pretty consistent about making good decisions and have no room to improve in your decision-making, then you can stop reading and give this book to someone else. If you do not identify with that previous statement, however, then you can benefit from being a more optimal decision maker. More specifically, this book is for the following people with these experiences:

- People who have difficulties making good decisions consistently.
- People who often feel rushed to do things impulsively because they feel the need to respond right away.

- People who often feel confused and stuck, which leads to inaction. Oftentimes, the problem gets worse.
- People who rarely communicate what they really think or feel but later feel resentful or sad for being left out.
- People who have the common experience of mediocre living and who fail to live up to their potential.
- Those who may seem to have many good things in their life and yet still feel like there is something missing, like there is an emptiness or a void inside.

If you can identify with one or more of these experiences, the Optimal Decision-Making Framework can help you overcome these challenges.

Here is what we will be exploring. Chapter 1 will deal with various types of indecision and why they occur. Chapter 2 will handle another equally dangerous phenomenon—poor decisions. In chapter 3, we will see how poor decisions can impact your life, and what cost you pay to make them. Chapter 4 is the first introduction to the Framework; we will explain its different components and offer you an overview. Chapters 5 to 10 will explore the Framework in depth, as well as explain how to implement it. And in the last chapter, chapter 11, we will tackle a crucial component of good decision-making: understanding that a bad decision is not the end of the line, and you can bounce back from negative outcomes.

This book does not guarantee perfection. You will still make mistakes. Knowing better does not always translate into doing better. Not knowing better, however, will often contribute into doing worse. Ignorance is not bliss if you want to be in control of your decisions. Sometimes we call a decision a "mistake" because it causes emotional discomfort, or because it has consequences we did not anticipate or like. Given that we are finite creatures, misfortune will happen at times. We must remember that it can be a blessing in disguise. It can be good for us when things do not go our way (though we certainly do not feel that way in the moment!). In fact, sometimes the wisdom from the "mistakes" may be necessary for a future win. Making mistakes is part of the process of becoming an optimal decision maker. That is the Framework mindset. The aim of the Framework is to empower you to make informed decisions. It will cultivate your ability to systematically think through your life decisions in an authentic manner and create positive outcomes.

Imagine becoming a person who is confident in making decisions. No matter how complicated or stressful a problem may be, you have this underlying inner peace because you know how to work through anything. You have a mental clarity that allows you to see things for what they really are and to know what options are available. You are attuned with your emotions and can quickly identify the need or want. Every decision you make can be linked to your values, and you can see how that contributes to your purpose. You are also able to identify the resistance to making the right decision and now possess the courage to overcome those barriers. This is what an optimal decision maker looks like. This can be you.

The question now is: "Are you ready to be a person who makes optimal decisions?" If your answer is yes, then it is time to learn more about why you make the decisions you do and how you can change them. It is time to shift to a Framework mindset.

THE FRAMEWORK

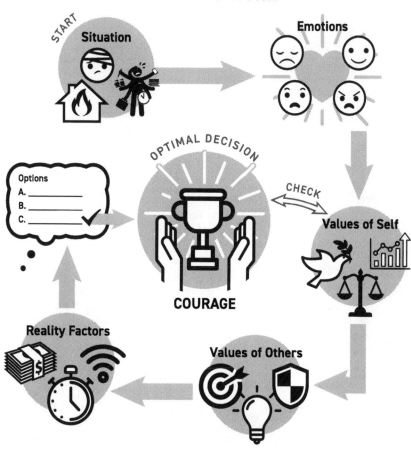

CHAPTER 1

I Don't Want to Be Wrong

Meet Bobby. He is your average guy who wants to be liked by other people. People generally think he is a nice guy, but he has a problem...he is too nice. That's right. He is the person who avoids conflict like the plague and rarely asserts himself. He is somewhat socially awkward and does not take a stance on anything. It can be something as simple as picking a place for lunch, but his default answer is often, "I don't know. Whatever you want." It is really hard not to like Bobby, but there is an uneasiness about him. He is clearly intelligent but seems to lack personality. No one really knows him.

The truth is that Bobby has opinions of his own. He can easily name a few restaurants. Just because he is a chill guy does not mean he has zero preferences! So why does he say he does not know? In case he picks the "wrong answer" and people will not like him. Bobby is scared of the drama. Logically, he knows that picking a place to eat is a little thing, yet emotionally he feels great resistance to choose.

One day, Bobby really wanted pizza but said, "I don't know. Whatever is okay."

His girlfriend, Tina, suggested, "How about Mexican food?"

Bobby's initial thought was, "Man, I really don't feel like Mexican food." What he said instead was, "Sure! That sounds good!" What a lie.

Since Tina was not a mind reader, she went ahead and replied, "Great! Let's go to Taqueria Los Gallos."

Then feelings of defeat and resentment started surfacing. Bobby had eaten Mexican food yesterday! He really did not want it again today. He tried not to let the decision bother him, but Tina noticed that Bobby's mood began shifting from being happy to being more reserved and irritable. She did not appreciate Bobby's vibe and wondered, "Is it something I said? Why is this happening again?" Fed up with Bobby's moodiness, Tina called off the lunch and broke up with him. Bobby did not assert himself in fear of disappointing her, and yet his accommodating answer not only disappointed her but also ended the relationship. Indecision does not neutralize situations. It leads to decisions being made for you—often undesirable ones. Indecision equates to a less-than-optimal life. If you can identify with some of these characteristics, we have a decision-making problem.

Why is making certain decisions so difficult? For starters, we have too many options. This may not be true in all situations, but our world has shifted into a consumer-centric society that caters to the individual. I call it the "Burger King problem" where everything follows Burger King's motto: "Have it your way." The myth is that the more options we have, the more satisfied we will be. Make a trip to Starbucks. Which drink would you like? Latte, cappuccino, espresso, or drip? Would you like it with soy milk, 2% milk, whole milk, almond milk, or oat milk? What kind of coffee would you like? Coffee beans from Asia, Latin America, or Africa? Or a blend of multiple beans? How would you like your coffee? Drip, pour over, blended, or regular? What temperature would you prefer? Piping hot, room temperature, or iced? You get the picture. As a non-coffee drinker, going to Starbucks can feel quite overwhelming! With such a pricey drink, I do not want to make the wrong choice. Is there a right choice? I will just get water...thanks.

Research shows that more options are not always better. Psychologist Sheena Iyengar and Mark Lepper (2000) did their Jam Study to see how many options of jams made available at a supermarket would actually convert to sales and satisfaction. The options of jam samples were two, six, 24, and 30. The assumption was that having 30 different options would lead to the most happiness, because there's a greater chance of there being a perfect jam for you. Instead, Iyengar and Lepper found that 30 different jams (as you can probably imagine) simply felt overwhelming. The people who purchased their jam after tasting many samples ended up with greater buyer's remorse. There was an increase in second-guessing themselves and thinking, "Maybe there was a better jam than the one I bought," which led to regret and dissatisfaction.[1]

I see many young adults with decision issues that extend beyond crafting the right drink or picking the preferred jam. They are worried about their future. I remember talking to my client, Dave, who is educated, financially resourced, and supported by his parents but paralyzed by fear when it comes to making a career choice. He knew that his initial choice in accounting was unfulfilling, so he made the bold decision to quit. Now there is a new level of pressure to pick the "right" job to

1   Iyengar, S. S. & Lepper, M. R. (2000). When choice is demotivating: Can one desire be too much of a good thing? *Journal of Personality and Social Psychology*, 79(6), 995–1006. https://doi.org/10.1037/0022-3514.79.6.995

avoid wasting more time and energy. He does not want to return to square one. Then there are Dave's parents, who are successful immigrant parents. They want him to take over the family business and settle down with a family friend's daughter (who they believe would bring honor to the family). Although he knows that this current life stage is not what he wants, he is unable to answer the question, "What do I want for my life?"

Let's talk about making the right call. What is right and wrong? Although it is not my role to dictate anyone's morality, we are essentially defining the best or optimal decision as the one that benefits us. That is probably how most people define what is "right." The tricky thing is that right and wrong seems to be fluid and contextual. Defining absolutes seems more and more difficult. What is right for you may not be right for the person next to you.

There was a time when we trusted institutions and authorities to define what was "right" for society. Life seemed "simpler" before, when there were well-defined rules of how we should live in order to be happy—do what the authorities say, and everyone will be content. But we now live in a postmodern society where people generally do not trust organizations to define what is right anymore. According to Edelman, a communications marketing firm, less than 30% of Americans trust the government compared to 75% in 1964.[2] The Barna Group in 2018 did research on Americans' perspectives on police brutality, and 53% agreed with the idea that "the police unfairly target people of color and other minority groups."[3] Then there is the loss of credibility in religious institutions with the sexual abuse of children by Catholic priests and accusations of sexual misconduct by mega church pastors. John Fea, a professor of American history at Messiah College, summed it up perfectly when he said, "I think we are living in an era when expertise and authority are under attack in a variety of areas, whether it be religion, politics, or academic life."[4]

So now there is no overarching idea of "right" to follow—a supposedly easy path to happiness. After the betrayal of trust by institutions and authorities, many people tried to define happiness for themselves. Happiness became the purpose for life. The only problem with that model was that happiness is an emotional state, which means it changes. One moment you are happy, and then

2   Pew Research Center (2015). *Beyond distrust: How Americans view their government*. https://www.people-press.org/2015/11/23/1-trust-in-government-1958-2015/
3   Barna Group. (2017). *Barna Trends 2018: What's new and what's next at the intersection of faith and culture*. Baker Publishing Group.
4   Jackson, G. P. (2019). The 7 people Christians trust more than their pastors. *Christianity Today*. https://www.christianitytoday.com/news/2019/january/gallup-pastor-clergy-trust-professions-poll.html

the next moment you feel disappointed. Imagine trying to play a game where the rules of how to win change every few minutes. Would you still play? Probably not, because it would be impossible to succeed. It would be senseless and frustrating. That is how people often play the game of life. People pursue goals they think will bring them happiness, only to find themselves unfulfilled. Perhaps happiness as an end goal is aiming too low. If happiness is not the goal, then what is the aim for life? We will unpack that more thoroughly when addressing our values.

Back to Dave's dilemma of making the right career choice. What makes his situation so daunting is his belief that making the wrong choice will be a permanent mark of failure on his life. There is so much pressure to be "perfect," because mistakes are perceived as a waste of time. Time does not stop for anybody. Everyone is allotted 24 hours a day, seven days a week, 365 days a year. That is a fact. When someone spends several years trying something that fails, those years of time, resources, and energy are gone with little to show for it. Then the failure gets internalized as being a failure as a person. That prospect freaks people out, which prevents them from making a decision unless they have a fail-proof strategy.

The truth is, there is rarely a fail-proof strategy. If you are looking for an answer that is "right," that has a 100% guarantee for success, stop. You are looking for a unicorn, a beautiful idea that is unobtainable. It does not exist. The only constant in life is change. There will always be risks to every decision you make. Looking for a perfect solution is a sure way to live a life filled with anxiety and stress.

Dave is paralyzed by his fear of making the "wrong" career choice, so he does not choose at all. Instead, this unspoken pressure to be perfect leads him toward creative ways to "deal" with the problem. The common strategies? Do not deal with it now. Procrastinate. Do not speak up. Pretend it is not a problem. The most famous one? Distractions. In our modern 21st century world, there are enough distractions to fill decades of time. Ever heard of Netflix? The Netflix CEO, Redd Hastings, admitted that the purpose of Netflix was to fight for your attention. Netflix's competitor? Sleep.[5] They do not want you to sleep! The system is created to begin the next TV episode or movie after a few-second countdown so you never have to stop. It is an easy and mindless escape from the hardships of decision-making. There are many other forms of distractions, such as alcohol, drugs, pornography, and fill-in-the-blank. These are disguised as freedom of choice, but they can turn into bondage when they take away from your best life.

---

5   Raphael, R. (2017). Netflix CEO Redd Hastings: Sleep is our competition. *Fast Company*. https://www.fastcompany. com/40491939/netflix-ceo-reed-hastings-sleep-is-our-competition

Then there are other, covert distractions that disguise themselves as "good" things. (As Jim Collins would say, "Good is the enemy of great.").[6] This may entail family obligations, career, exercise, charity, selfless giving, and self-care. These are even more insidious simply because very few people can call you out on it. Although these activities are not inherently evil, they can be used to shrink away from addressing important issues and needs. They can keep you from living your best life.

Dave's problem is a fear of failure (notice it is the fear rather than the failure itself!). But there are other fears and barriers that can keep us from living our authentic lives. Fear of rejection is a big factor, especially social rejection. We know that humans are psychologically wired to be in relationships and belong to communities. Kross, Berman, Mischel, Smith, and Wager (2011) found that the brain interprets and experiences social rejection as pain similar to physical harm.[7] The saying, "It breaks my heart" may be more than just a metaphor. So we go out of our way to avoid that feeling to keep ourselves safe

---

6   Collins, J. (2001). *Good to great: Why some companies make the leap and others don't.* HarperCollins Publishers.

7   Kross, E., Berman, M. G., Mischel, W., Smith, E. E., & Wager, T. D. (2011). Social rejection shares somatosensory representations with physical pain. https://www.pnas.org/content/pnas/108/15/6270.full.pdf

from disapproval and exclusion. This leads to a lack of transparency and vulnerability.

For example, as an Asian American, I know my ethnic roots include concepts such as "losing face," false humility, and dishonor. These concepts prevent people from showing up and communicating honestly. Robert Neelly Bellah (1975) described the philosophy of Confucianism as being more than just a philosophy or religion.[8] It is a way of living interwoven into the everyday fabric of life. In this way of living, there are acceptable values and norms for each person, strictly defined according to their social hierarchy and role. This is why there are certain obligations that must be fulfilled regardless of how you actually think or feel about them.

Although my parents were somewhat Westernized after their move to America, there is still an understanding that I present myself in the most proper way. I should appear to have everything together in public, lest I bring shame to my family. I am not my own but an extension of the "greater whole." The collective or tribe mentality can be positive in that it keeps me accountable to others. It requires that I am thoughtful and considerate of how my actions may affect my loved ones. But it can also

---

8   Bellah, R. N. (1975). *The broken covenant: American civil religion in a time of trial.* Seabury Press.

discourage me from being honest when things seem anything short of being "picture perfect."

A lack of transparency and vulnerability is not an Asian thing. It is a human thing. I have seen clients across multiple races and cultures who experience similar realities. McGoldrick, Giordano, and Garcia-Preto (2005) highlighted a few cultural dynamics that may keep people from being more honest. In the Hispanic or Latinx culture, there is the concept of machismo, where the "man's man" displays only strength and aggression because anything other than anger would mean the man is weak. There is also simpatia or smooth relationships, a concept that aims to avoid conflict at all cost. In the African American culture, there is a huge taboo about seeking therapy. It is believed that private matters that occur in the home should stay in the home. There is resistance to discussing painful parts of one's story due to a distrust of institutions and negative experiences created by social, economic, and political oppression. Those of Arabic descent shy away from the stigma of "psychological problems" and therefore emotional challenges are less likely to be discussed. The social fear of showing up in a real way is a human condition that supersedes any one particular culture.[9]

---

9 McGoldrick, M., Giordano, J., & Garcia-Preto, N. (2005). *Ethnicity & family therapy*. Guilford Press.

Even as a psychologist, I have challenges sharing how I really feel and think with certain people, which stems from my childhood. Growing up in an Asian immigrant household, I had seasons of confusion sorting out my authentic self. Am I American? Chinese? Taiwanese? Something in between? There was a cultural expectation from my father's upbringing to "respect your elders," which meant that my voice did not matter to him. Although my relationship with my father has significantly improved, I was genuinely scared to be vulnerable with him. There was little room for dialogue, because "he is the father, so therefore, he is always right." He seemed quick to judge, and his short temper made him emotionally unsafe. To prevent potential anger outbursts and punishment, I learned to tell him what he wanted to hear, and I omitted what was "nonessential" information. A sad truth is that not every person is trustworthy and safe to be real around. The real tragedy, however, is when that causes you to be dishonest with yourself. Your voice does matter, and it is time to take yourself seriously.

Remember that while social rejection causes pain, not all pain is bad for you. There are times when pain and discomfort are the result of personal growth. It is difficult for people to see that, however. Most people subconsciously interpret pain as being solely bad. But pain is a natural part of life, and there are times when we must accept it so we can become our better, truer selves.

CONCLUSION

Indecision is just a decision being made for you. You are opting to be voiceless and powerless, hoping the outcome will miraculously turn in your favor. It is allowing confusion or discomfort to take over your thinking. It is giving your power away. Sometimes, indecision is disguised as "open mindedness" or "being nice" when the reality is more about shrinking away from responsibility and dishonoring yourself. Other times, we truly believe the decision is of our own making when unconscious or societal factors are actually misleading us to choose inauthentically. It is time to wake up and see what is really informing our decisions!

Remember Bobby? After working with Bobby in counseling, he experienced an inner transformation that began by identifying his fears and working through them. Bobby was able to be really honest with himself about what he wanted in life. He started owning his decisions, one at a time. He utilized the Framework to clarify his decision-making.

I realized this transformation occurred when he started talking differently. He seemed to sit up straighter. There were less hesitations and unnecessary apologies. Bobby would look me in the eyes with a newfound confidence and courage that he never experienced before. He was still a nice guy but now his niceness was not a symptom of his fear or weakness, but rather a respectful boldness. Bobby knew what was important to him, and he made decisions that reflected his values. As a natural by-product, he experienced more happiness and a sense of inner peace.

Now suppose Bobby decided not to become an optimal decision maker. His life may have taken a very different turn. He would most likely be stuck with the pain of being overlooked and insecure. Some of you may be thinking, "Okay, so what? I don't want to speak up about what restaurant I want to eat at. I genuinely don't care." How you do anything is how you do everything. The small decisions in your life reflect how you will make bigger decisions. There may be a tendency to downplay the seriousness of indecision. Indecision is not a victimless crime. What if indecision can actually kill off everything important to you? Indecision is not an innocent little problem. It has the potential to suck the soul out of your existence.

There is another type of decision that is as destructive as indecision, and that is making poor decisions. In the next chapter, we will explore what poor decisions look like and why they may happen.

CHAPTER 2

Why Poor Decisions Happen

"Oops, I did it again!"

That is not only a Britney Spears line.[10] It is a feeling many of us are familiar with after we make the same bad choices again and again. The conventional wisdom is to learn from our mistakes, remember the pain, and do better next time. But Nikolova, Lamberton, and Haws (2016) found that people who have a higher rate of recalling their failures are actually more likely to fail again.[11] How counterintuitive! We criticize and punish

---

10   Spears, B. (2000) Oops!... I did it again [Song]. On *Oops!... I did it again* [Album]. Jive Records.

11   Nikolova, H., Lamberton, C., & Haws, K. (2015, June 30). Haunts or helps from the past: Understanding the effect of...

ourselves in hopes of learning from the pain, but some-how that is a fruitless strategy. More often than not, our self-blame just fuels low self-esteem, and low self-esteem leads to more poor decisions. It is a vicious cycle of pain. For many people, the issue is not a lack of knowledge. It is being unable to understand and break out of the cycle, resulting in doing the same stupid thing one more time. You have experienced these devastating consequences before. You know how the story ends. Yet, here you are, in the same place again.

Meet Jack. He is a newly divorced man who has a lot to lose as a father of two. Jack loves his kids more than anything in the world. He is supposed to stay clean from drinking alcohol in order to gain custody of his kids. Jack knows that drinking is going to make the court rule unfa-vorably toward him. His ex-wife is with her new boyfriend and neglects the kids. Yet, he finds himself staring at his usual Suntory whiskey bottle again. When the pain is too great, and the stress feels overwhelming, alcohol gives him that emotional break. There are bills to pay and he cannot afford to lose his job. Yet the pain is just overbear-ing and the impulse to drink hits him hard. "Maybe just

---

...recall on current self-control. Retrieved November 18, 2020, from https://www.sciencedirect.com/science/article/abs/pii/ S1057740815000728.

one drink. I deserve a break. I already worked 12 hours today, and I want to relax." Before you know it, Jack drinks the rest of the bottle and does not remember how he ended up passed out on the floor. Same song, different tune. He hates himself when he drinks, yet he finds himself doing it again and again.

In the last chapter, we talked about indecision and some of the reasons why people are paralyzed by their choices. But it is not just indecision that harms a person. Making poor decisions can also sabotage one's future. These decisions can be rash. It is the mindset of "Forget this, I am going to quit this miserable job." In your self-righteous fury, you curse out the boss, relish in the five minutes of satisfaction, and then completely regret the decision when you need a letter of recommendation from your last employer. Thoughtless decisions such as this are strongly fueled by emotions. "If it feels right, then it must be real, and therefore the authentic me should act upon it." These decisions always "feel" right, until reality smacks you in the face and you end up in a worse situation.

The more extreme examples of poor decisions are people who feel so hopeless that suicide seems to be the only way out. When Kevin Hines and Ken Baldwin jumped off the Golden Gate Bridge, they immediately regretted their decision, even as they were falling. Luckily, they survived to tell the tale.[12] Others who have attempted suicide on the bridge have not been so lucky. They ended up being paralyzed from the neck down and they are still alive. According to the New England Journal of Medicine, as many as 33% to 80% of all suicide attempts are impulsive, and 90% of people who survive suicide attempts do not attempt suicide later.[13] As much as someone may want the pain to stop or the problems to go away, suicide is not the answer.

Then there are those poor decisions we know are bad, but that we cannot seem to walk away from. Meet Bruce. On the surface, this guy seems to have it all. He is married to his lovely wife, has two well-behaved kids, owns several profitable businesses, has a nice house, and a group of close friends. Bruce appears to have obtained the American dream and people look up to him. But Bruce also lives a secret life that very few people know about. Every few days, he gets drawn into partying with his old friends. It starts with a few drinks but leads to heavy alcohol consumption and cocaine. Bruce feels a

---

12   Friend, T. (2003). Jumpers: The fatal grandeur of the Golden Gate Bridge. *The New Yorker*. https://www.newyorker.com/magazine/2003/10/13/jumpers

13   Adwar, C. (2014). The role of impulsiveness is one of the saddest things about suicide. *Business Insider*. https://www.businessinsider.com/many-suicides-are-based-on-an-impulsive-decision-2014-8

need to maintain his persona as the "fun guy who doesn't give a damn" with these old friends, yet his evening ritual leaves him hungover and useless the next day. His wife gets very upset with his behavior, and his marriage is a few bad decisions away from a divorce. The truth is, Bruce has fought hard to be successful, but he still feels like something is missing in his life. The party lifestyle is his attempt to fill his need for excitement, but it never addresses the void. Bruce wants to be a man of integrity and a role model for his family, yet he cannot seem to stop these vices. His struggle for "freedom" only leaves him feeling more frustrated and emptier.

Jack and Bruce know their habits are bad for them. They both want to break out of their cycles. But they keep making bad decisions that lead them down the same paths. To a lesser degree, this is our story too. We all have bad habits. Vices. Things you know are unhealthy but you continue doing anyway. The author of Proverbs 26:11 gives this explicit illustration: "As a dog returns to his vomit, so a fool repeats his folly." Some people may call it an addiction and say they cannot help it. I am not here to minimize the issue of addictions, biological factors, and the implications on the brain. But the reality is that, at some point, the reasons no longer matter. Even if you have the most legitimate explanations for poor choices, the consequences do not care. You still pay the price.

In this chapter, we will explore the many answers to the million-dollar question: why do people make bad decisions? There is no single, comprehensive answer to this question. Poor decisions sprout from many factors, both contextual and psychological. I have listed the most important factors in the following sections. As you read, look for those causes that resonate with you. Remember, awareness is the first step to change.

PSYCHOLOGICAL NEEDS

All people have needs. There are legitimate needs that must be fulfilled for our life's work, and then there are counterfeit "needs" that cause more harm than good. Counterfeit needs contribute to poor decision-making. I learned of these "needs" in a leadership development training by Klemmer and Associates, and they really changed my perspective. Now, I am sharing them with you. According to Brian Klemmer, there are three major psychological needs that get people in trouble:[14]

1. **The need to be right.** This is that strong, nagging pull in your gut that urges you to spew that verbal

---

14   Klemmer, B. (2005). *If how-to's were enough we would all be skinny, rich, & happy*. Insight.

comeback. It is the need to persuade or prove to another person that you are right and they are wrong. It is unhealthy pride. Sometimes, it is not good enough for you to know that you are right. You want *other* people to acknowledge you are right. This is at the heart of most arguments and fights. "I am right and this is the only way to see it." The need to be right has caused ruptures in friendships, initiated divorces, and even started world wars. Have you ever fought with a spouse or friend, chosen not to speak to each other for days, and later forgot the reason for the fight? It is our innate craving for our version of justice at the cost of the relationship.

2. **The need to look good.** Sure, you can call it vanity but this is a different expression of unhealthy pride. Some people fear public speaking more than death. Why? They do not want to look stupid. There is such a fear of social disapproval and rejection that people make all sorts of inauthentic choices to appear acceptable. Social media is full of these cases. People post pictures they want other people to see to brand themselves in a favorable way, even to the point where the picture is clearly photoshopped and fake!

The need to look good keeps people from being real and is seen in a life-giving way. Timothy Keller wrote, "To be loved but not known is comforting but superficial. To be known and not loved is our greatest fear. But to be fully known and truly loved is, well, a lot like being loved by God. It is what we need more than anything. It liberates us from pretense, humbles us out of our self-righteousness, and fortifies us for any difficulty life can throw at us" (Keller, 2016).[15] We all want to be seen and loved for who we are, but we are too deathly afraid that people will reject us if they really knew us. That is what keeps people from showing up and causes them to feel invisible most of their lives.

3. **The cycle of the three Rs: Resentment, Resistance, Revenge.** We enter this destructive cycle whenever people offend us. It comes from a legitimate need for justice, but it is expressed in an unhealthy way. For example, an employee gets humiliated by his manager at a meeting. He is pissed off but does not want to speak up because he will lose his job. Subconsciously, he begins to disengage

---

15 Keller, T., & Keller, K. (2016). *The meaning of marriage: Facing the complexities of commitment with the wisdom of God.* Penguin Books.

from his work, and he creates emotional distance. He finds ways to avoid the manager, and he looks away whenever they run into each other. His resentment builds up over time, and he cannot help but notice all the reasons his manager is a bad person. One day, he notices his boss being robbed in a nearby alleyway. Instead of calling the police, he turns the other way because he thinks, "My boss is finally getting what he deserves." When he learns that his boss got seriously injured, he is filled with guilt and wonders how he turned into such a callous person. In the name of conscious or unconscious justice, people's lives get reorganized into the three Rs and they become driven by negativity.

EROS AND THANATOS

There are other inner forces that encourage poor decision-making. Sigmund Freud theorized that people have both life instincts (Eros) and death instincts (Thanatos).[16] Although there is little scientific evidence to support this

---

16 Cherry, K. (2020). *Freud's theories of life and death instincts*. Very Well Mind. https://www.verywellmind.com/life-and-death-instincts-2795847

idea, the concept characterizes internal conflict quite well. Freud postulated that there are life instincts that motivate us to survive, seek pleasure, and reproduce. We are usually aware of these life instincts that drive us to be "selfish" in the name of self-preservation. Freud also proposed an opposing force that is driven by death and largely subconscious. This force can manifest as destructive tendencies toward other people (e.g., aggression, violence) or it can manifest against ourselves (e.g., excessive drinking, promiscuous sexual relationships, reckless driving, suicide). The Thanatos instinct is especially prevalent when times get hard. The reality of existence contains pain and suffering. It is a theme that is universally present in all world religions and existential philosophies. I will admit the idea that I would be so peaceful if my life simply ceased has crossed my mind during stressful moments. You can imagine how much more intense Thanatos would be for someone struggling with depression and suicidal thoughts. This kind of instinct can unconsciously lead people to make poor decisions. It reminds me of Molly, a 60-year-old patient, who was diagnosed with depression and diabetes for most of her life. She did not really want to die, but she did not really want to live. Her way of conforming to her death instinct was to stop taking her insulin. Her thought was: "If it happens to be my time to go, I would be okay with it."

HYPOTHETICAL FUTURES

Humans tend to be opportunistic. We naturally try to optimize our actions by strategizing better ways to do things. This may lead us to second-guess our decisions or imagine alternative futures and possibilities. Schacter, Benoit, and Szpunar (2017) defined the term episodic future thinking as "the capacity to imagine or simulate events that might occur in one's personal future."[17] Schacter and Addis (2007) proposed the constructive episodic simulation hypothesis where people use past experiences and concepts to create future simulations.[18] It is like our brain is imagining a better outcome than the one we have now.

This becomes a bigger issue when our brain comes up with better outcomes that are based on fantasy, not facts. Memory is fluid and people can easily remember things wrong or misattribute causation to events. Take me, for example. I have a confession: sometimes, I have random

17 Schacter D. L., Benoit, R. G., & Szpunar, K. K. (2017). Episodic future thinking: Mechanisms and functions. *Curr Opin Behav Sci.* 17, 41–50. https://doi:10.1016/j.cobeha.2017.06.002

18 Schacter, D. L., Addis, D. R., Hassabis, D., Martin, V. C., Spreng, R. N., & Szpunar, K. K. (2012). The future of memory: remembering, imagining, and the brain. *Neuron*, 76(4), 677–694. https://doi.org/10.1016/j.neuron.2012.11.001

thoughts about my ex-girlfriends. I wonder how they are doing and how my life would be if I had married them instead of my wife. It seems absurd to me, because the love for my wife is strong, and I do not want to be with anyone else! But if this fantasy thinking about a "better life" remains in my unconscious, my decisions may be made based on inaccurate information and I would be worse off. You hear these stories about men going through their midlife crisis and divorcing their wife to be with 20-something-year-old secretaries, regretting it later because their shallow assumptions did not produce deeper fulfillment.

People are poor predictors of the future and thus bad decisions are often based on the fears of "what if." Psychologists Dan Gilbert and Tim Wilson studied people's tendencies to do affective forecasting, which is predicting how people would feel if something good or bad would happen; often predicting inaccurately.[19] The general trend is that good things do not feel good for long and bad things do not feel bad for long either. Common examples are people who win the lottery, individuals who become paralyzed after an accident, and assistant

---

19   Wilson, T. D., & Gilbert, D. T. (2005). Affective forecasting: Knowing what to want. *Current Directions in Psychological Science*, 14(3), 131–134. https://doi.org/10.1111/j.0963-7214.2005.00355.x

professors receiving tenure; they all return to a general baseline of happiness in a relatively short period of time. The problem is that many people focus too heavily on how one particular event will feel and therefore avoid making important decisions. In fact, many people create worst-case scenarios in their mind and respond as if it occurred already. We actively think how our actions will utterly fail and how terrible it would be. Or something irreversibly terrible will occur if we actually shared our truth with someone we loved. So, if we are so terrible at predicting the future, should we form our important decisions based on these predictions? Probably not.

SELF-SABOTAGE

Self-sabotage is when people consciously or unconsciously act to derail their own success. There is no one to blame but themselves. Self-sabotaging behaviors feel like we are purposely making bad choices to hurt ourselves. Think of the common saying: "I am my own worst enemy." Is this not often the case? We are unnecessarily critical and twice as mean to ourselves than we would ever be to our friends. This counterintuitive phenomenon of self-sabotage happens to many of my clients. They start making good decisions and experience a little success, but ultimately they do something to mess it all up.

Consider our friend Jack, for example (you met him at the beginning of the chapter). He finally gets sober from alcohol and nominated for a promotion at work, only to get drunk the night before his interview. Does this sound familiar? The million-dollar question is "Why?" Why would any rational, happiness-desiring person stop themselves from experiencing success? Even worse, why would people be the cause of their own unhappiness, ruin healthy relationships, lose their jobs, and forfeit everything precious to them?

Obviously, this is a psychologically complicated question with no simple answer. Through my experience working with numerous clients, I have observed a few trends that may help explain why some people carry out self-defeating behaviors.

The Unconscious Fear of Success

Being successful looks great on the surface but comes with its costs. People say they want to be successful, but their words do not always match their behaviors. I like the saying: "If the grass is greener on the other side of the fence, you can bet the water bill is higher." Or another version of that quote is: "The grass is greener where you water it."

Think about what success means to you. For many people, success may mean more money, accomplishments, recognition, and acceptance by others. Although success seems to be the stuff of happiness, it often comes with more responsibility, more demands, and more stress. With increased territory comes more potential headaches to manage that increase. There is more gain to lose. People often believe that having enough success will bring the happiness and peace they are looking for, and yet the opposite is often true: people with more success are more anxious and paranoid about losing it. Actor Jim Carrey stated: "I think everybody should get rich and famous and do everything they ever dreamed of so they can see that it's not the answer."[20] Often, fears and insecurities lead to behaviors that end the success in order to avoid the burdens associated with it. For some people, they reject success and fail on purpose to get out of the "rat race."

In some ways, people are afraid of success because showing up in their power feels unfamiliar and scary. It is as author Marianne Williamson famously said:

Our deepest fear is not that we are inadequate. Our deepest fear is that we are powerful beyond measure.

---

20   Absolute Motivation (n.d.) *Home* [YouTube channel],
      retrieved November 18, 2020, https://www.youtube.com/
      watch?v=wTblBYqQQag

It is our light, not our darkness that most frightens us. We ask ourselves, "Who am I to be brilliant, gorgeous, talented, and fabulous?" Actually, who are you not to be? You are a child of God. Your playing small does not serve the world. There is nothing enlightened about shrinking so that other people will not feel insecure around you. We are all meant to shine, as children do. We were born to make manifest the glory of God that is within us. It is not just in some of us; it is in everyone and when we let our own light shine, we unconsciously give others permission to do the same. As we are liberated from our own fear, our presence automatically liberates others.[21]

That is the power of embracing authenticity—by choosing not to self-sabotage, we can allow our success to manifest in a real way.

Dysfunction and Failure Feel Normal

Many people grow up around hurt people who, in turn, hurt them. This hurt can range from neglect to traumatic abuse. People who go through this often see those experiences as "normal." They get used to the dysfunction

---

21   Williamson, M. (2015). *A return to love: Reflections on the principles of a course in miracles.* Thorsons Classics

and have learned ways to survive these stressors. There is a strange illusion of control in unhealthy relationships because "I am familiar with bad behaviors and know how to respond." When the same person encounters a healthy person or situation, a newfound distress occurs because "it does not feel right." It feels like a loss of control. Unconsciously, people will date or befriend toxic people while pushing away healthy people to put themselves in a familiar situation again...often to their own detriment. Like the Irish proverb suggests: "Better the devil you know than the devil you don't."[22] Instead of creating opportunities for something better, the fear of the unknown pushes people to return to the familiar dysfunction despite the pain.

The Lack of Self-Love and Acceptance

Self-sabotaging behaviors may also originate from disliking oneself. Negative experiences paired with self-blame can create a general sense of "never being good enough." Constantly feeling devalued creates an internal message that "I don't matter and therefore I don't deserve good things." People draw this conclusion because of

22 Merriam-Webster. (n.d.). Better the devil you know than the devil you don't idiom. https://www.merriam-webster.com/ dictionary/better%20the%20devil%20you%20know%20 than%20the%20devil%20you%20don%27t

their strong need for congruency. This means the way
they feel within themselves needs to match their external reality. If there is a mismatch, then something has to
change to regain congruency. For example, a boy with a
healthy sense of self gets told, "You are a loser." The boy
may feel hurt by the criticism but he is able to tell himself, "That is just not true. Clearly she is a mean person."
His self-perception is positive, so her negative statement
did not match his internal reality. He draws the conclusion that the negative external feedback corresponds to
the unpleasant person, and he stops interacting with
her. If the same boy had poor self-esteem, being called a
loser gets personal. His sustained emotional pain occurs
because she highlighted the insecurity that he already
believed about himself. Similarly, people who do not love
themselves cannot take pleasure in positive experiences
for a prolonged time, because that external reality does
not match their undesirable sense of self. Unconscious
self-sabotaging thoughts and behaviors create the negativity that matches their inner world.

Avoidance of Discomfort

The desire for instant gratification and the avoidance of
discomfort can also lead to poor decisions. I worked with
a client named Diana who was quite successful in her
career. She was a manager of an auditing firm and did

well financially. Diana was distressed with her inability to follow through with healthy decisions. She wasted a lot of time at home. As we explored her life further, we realized that she avoided anything that made her uncomfortable. Literally everything. Mail stacked up on her table. Her sink was overflowing with dishes. Her rationale would be "I already worked a long day, so I'll do it later." Later never came, until her boyfriend got upset with her. Diana procrastinated with work by spending countless hours taking naps or scrolling through social media. She avoided physical exercise and ate junk food because it was easy and comfortable. Despite her logical brain telling her to grow up, she could not seem to make decisions that were good for her.

Many poor decisions are inadequately processed emotional decisions that cause ruptures in relationships. Problems often cause distressing feelings, such as powerlessness and anxiety. Without fully understanding why, more "powerful" actions become default to ward off the discomfort. How many people act out their anger only to regret what they said or did after cooling down? There is this myth that living and behaving based on how we feel is being the "real me." Using our emotions as our only indicator of authenticity is like the ancient Indian parable of the Blind Men and the Elephant. Each blind man is touching only one part of the elephant (e.g., the rough trunk, the brush-like tail, the flappy ears, the smooth tusks) and describing the entire animal based on that part.[23] It is comical because each blind man is right about their part yet inaccurately seeing the elephant. Emotions are only one part of the equation. They are a very important part, which is why chapter 5 is dedicated to emotions, but not enough to make optimal decisions.

Fear of Loss

People are typically risk aversive, which means decisions lean toward minimizing loss, just like monkeys. Chen, Lakshminarayanan, and Santos (2006) discovered that capuchin monkeys have an intrinsic instinct for avoiding loss. In one of the experiments, a monkey was given a token to exchange for apple slices. If the token was given to the female experimenter, she would give the monkey one apple slice. If the token was given to the male experimenter, he would display two apple slices, remove one of the slices from the dish, and give one apple slice to the monkey. The other monkeys saw that both experimenters gave only one apple slice per token. Logically, the monkeys should not care which experimenter exchanged

---

23 Peace Corps. (n.d.). A folk tale from India that teaches intercultural awareness by illustrating how different perspectives lead to distinct points of view. https://www.peacecorps.gov/educators/resources/story-blind-men-and-elephant/

the apple slices with their tokens, right? Wrong. Seventy-nine percent of the monkeys chose to exchange their token with the female experimenter![24] We also make decisions based on perceived loss even if it does not make objective sense!

Social psychology has identified a few human tendencies that keep us from taking necessary risks. Daniel Kahneman, Jack Knetsch, and Richard Thaler highlighted a few of these cognitive biases that make people more irrational than rational. The Endowment Effect, for example, is when people have a tendency to irrationally overvalue something they already possess, because there is an emotional attachment of ownership to it. In fact, people tend to feel twice the amount of pain when they lose that possession compared to the pleasure of gaining it for the first time. This was illustrated in an experiment where Kahneman and his researchers divided participants into buyers and sellers. The sellers were given coffee mugs and asked what their price would be to sell their mugs. Kahneman's team found that the sellers placed a much higher price on their mug compared to what the buyers perceived the mug to be worth. The Framing

---

24   Chen M. K, Lakshminarayanan V., Santos, L. R. (2006).
     How basic are behavioral biases? Evidence from capuchin
     monkey trading behavior. *J. Political Econ.* 114, 517–537. https://
     doi:10.1086/503550

Effect is when people tend to respond more favorably to taking risks when a situation is framed in a positive way compared to a negative way despite the message being exactly the same. For example, people are more likely to support an opportunity to save 90 out of 100 lives instead of proposing the risk of losing 10 out of 100 lives or agree to using a 95% effective condom rather than a 5% ineffective condom. It is interesting to note that the Framing Effect increases as people get older and they generally become more risk aversive. Lastly, there is the classic loss aversion itself, where people are more motivated to keep from losing something rather than to gain something of equal value. Similar to the Endowment Effect, people feel twice the psychological pain of loss compared to the pleasure of gaining the same thing.[25] For example, Tversky and Kahneman gave participants the option of accepting a bet based on a coin toss. The participants would lose $100 if the coin flipped tails, but they would win $200 if the coin flipped heads. Although the statistical odds were 50-50, people needed the gains to be one and one-half to two times greater in order to move forward with the bet.[26]

---

25   Kahneman, D., Knetsch, J. L., & Thaler, R. H. (1991). Anomalies: The endowment effect, loss aversion, and status quo bias. *Journal of Economic Perspectives*, 5(1), 193–206.

26   Kahneman, D., & Tversky, A. (1979). *Prospect theory: An analysis of decision under risk*. National Emergency Training Center.

People can become quite irrational when there is a possibility of loss. Our brains are wired to keep us from any conceivable loss despite the possibility of gain. It seems that any type of change is interpreted cautiously as "bad." It goes with Bert Lance's saying: "If it ain't broke, don't fix it."[27] People do not want to make things worse. That is what keeps us from making decisions that may cause change...even if they are good things! Living a life of avoiding discomfort will not guarantee comfort. By the time something breaks, it may be too costly to repair. A risk-free life will ultimately lead to mediocrity and dissatisfaction.

CONCLUSION

As you can see, people make poor decisions for a variety of reasons. Some of these reasons are conscious, but many are largely unconscious. If you want to stop making poor decisions, it is important to start by shifting those unconscious reasons into the conscious. It is necessary to be *aware*. We cannot defeat the unseen "monster" in our mind. Many times, the monster seems overwhelming and

---

27   Schudel, M. (2013). Bert Lance, banker, and Carter, budget director. *The Washington Post*. https://www.washingtonpost.com/politics/bert-lance-banker-and-carter-budget-director/2013/08/16/a200f4f8-0689-11e3-9259-e2aafe5a5f84_story.html

scary because our imagination creates "worst-case scenarios" that are often untrue. By identifying the unconscious barriers and bringing them into consciousness, we have a fighting chance to address them properly. Even *when* (not *if*) you make another poor choice, a huge step toward optimal decision-making is to do it "on purpose." No more accidents. Decrease the surprises. As the wise Yoda from *Star Wars* said, "Do or do not, there is no try." Poor decisions will no longer just happen. Our intention is to make conscious decisions. It is time to step into our power and become mindful decision makers.

Remember, being a poor decision maker is not a moral failing or character flaw. It is a skill deficit. People who make poor decisions are often perceived as bad people. Or there is an assumption that bad things happen only to people who deserve it—something about karma? I do not believe this is true at all! Good things happen to both good and bad people. Bad things happen to both good and bad people. Good people make mistakes too! Researchers have found that most of our decisions are made unconsciously. In a way, all decisions are made on autopilot unless we intentionally do otherwise. Poor decisions can be made without our awareness. They do not make us bad people, and they do not mean we deserve bad things.

Instead, it simply means we can do better. And when people *know* better, they are more likely to *do* better. Dr.

Ross Greene, a child psychologist, has a philosophy that "Kids do well if they can."[28] I have asked hundreds of kids the question: "Would you rather get straight As or straight Fs in school?" I have never met a kid who said, "Yes, give me those Fs!" Every kid wants to be successful. So why are they not? The underlying philosophy is that kids are not successful because there is a gap or missing skill that prevents them from getting to where they want to be. This is equally true about bad decisions. There is a missing Framework where people lack the skills to make optimal decisions. I will teach you that Framework skill in the upcoming chapters so you can become an optimal decision maker. In both a literal and figurative sense, your life depends on it.

---

28   Greene, R. W. (2014). *The explosive child: A new approach for understanding and parenting easily frustrated, chronically inflexible children.* Harper.

CHAPTER 3

The High Cost of Inauthentic Decisions

I looked straight at my parents and lied with a smile. I knew it was wrong but found myself doing it again. Then again. Toward the end, I hardly recognized myself. The choices I made to gain the approval of another person came at the cost of my own integrity. My decisions were no longer authentic, and I lost respect for myself.

It started with Sally. I met her during my senior year of high school. She was from another high school and the cousin of someone in my speech and debate class. When Sally came into the room, the world seemed to freeze. She had this charisma and confidence that drew me in like a moth to a flame. Sally was beautiful, sweet, and intelligent. She even had her own car! I definitely wanted to be her friend. We clicked immediately and the chemistry was intense. On the phone, she told me, "If we aren't officially dating, then we should stop talking to each other." I had always imagined myself asking the girl out (I know, call me old-fashioned) and, in my gut, I now felt pressured to ask her out. It was only our second conversation! Yet I did not want our interaction to end, so I agreed to be her boyfriend.

Then my integrity got hijacked toward a path of depravity. Sally was very thoughtful and frequently surprised me with romantic gestures like leaving a note in my locker or bringing me a gift. Then she passive aggressively communicated my need to do the same. Again, I felt the pressure to prove my love to her with romantic feats. The expectation seemed to get higher and grander the next go-around. The relationship began feeling like a chore, and my anxiety rose as I tried to think of what to do next. Nothing I did seemed good enough for her.

Then Sally began pushing the envelope. She would make a "request" that both of us knew was wrong. She asked me to sneak out of my house to watch the sunrise. Then she asked me to hang out and "study" at her place. We pushed physical boundaries. Sally lied to her parents too. Once we started the pattern of lying to our parents, it was difficult to stop. I will admit, it was exciting but in a criminal way. What killed me on the inside was the betrayal of my parents. My parents had such a strong trust in me and never questioned my motives. I also saw myself as being an honest person, but not anymore. My guilt consumed me and my heart felt calloused. I knew the relationship was no longer healthy, but I did not have the courage to end it. Our relationship almost ended when Sally asked me to sleep over. Her parents were out of town and I lied to get myself there. Long story short, her little sister told her parents, and we got caught a couple days after the incident. Her parents demanded an in-person apology, and I needed my parents to take me to her house. I was deeply ashamed and humiliated. Our parents told us to break up. We tried but got back together a month later.

Finally, Sally broke up with me. To be honest, I was somewhat relieved but shocked when I heard her reasoning. She ended the relationship because "You did everything I asked." I was very confused. I broke my moral code to please her and it was still my fault? She confessed, "I knew my ideas were kind of crazy, but you never stopped me." In hindsight, I know what she meant. By being her yes man, she could not trust me to protect her and do the right thing. In my effort to avoid disappointing her, I gave up my integrity and still lost the relationship.

There are moments when we experience the pressure to conform. We do what other people want to gain their approval. Do not stir up conflict. Keep the peace at all costs. Over time, you lose your sense of self. Self-confidence erodes and you can no longer distinguish your own voice from that of others. That is the aftermath of living for other people. Plato believed "The unexamined life is not worth living."[29] Why? Because you are no longer the driver but a passenger of your own life. Our life becomes an accumulation of automatic reactions. We stop thinking for ourselves. How do you live an unhappy and unfulfilling life? By living for the approval of other people. Your life goals may come from parents or what society deems is good for you. Is that the life you really want?

Imagine everything you could ever want being on top of a castle. You put your long ladder against the wall of the castle and begin climbing. After many years of blood, sweat, and tears, you reach the top of your castle wall only to realize, "This is the wrong castle!" What a tragedy. It is like a climber who toiled to scale Mt. Everest only to be surprised that the snow on top is the same as the snow from the bottom. Many celebrities and athletes become depressed after achieving fame and fortune

29   Baggini. J. (2005). Wisdom's folly. *The Guardian.* https://www.theguardian.com/theguardian/2005/may/12/features11.g24

because those things did not bring fulfillment. It is not what they really wanted. And in this pursuit of things that do not matter to you, what will you never get back? The time and energy to put toward the things that actually matter. What if you were able to identify the right castle before you started climbing? Even if it took you extra time to gain more clarity, would that be worth saving yourself years of fruitlessness? Work smarter, not harder! Identifying what truly matters to you in life is essential to optimal decision-making.

The cost of inauthentic decisions—decisions that do not truly align with who you are and what you value—is living an insignificant life. Sometimes, people only pursue small goals because they are easy, but it puts a ceiling on their potential. This is known as "playing it safe" or "playing not to lose." People stick to what they know despite being discontented with their current standing. My favorite barber illustrates this mindset. He is highly skilled in his craft but stays working for a company that treats him poorly with inadequate wages. How do I know? I hear him complain about it during every one of my haircuts. Why does he stay? He tells me, "At least I know the paycheck is guaranteed and my family gets health insurance." Apparently, his paycheck is not even guaranteed because his hours get cut randomly! When we talk about starting his own hairstyling business, he tells me all the reasons why it cannot be done. "It is hard to find a spot. Renting a place is too expensive. What if there aren't enough customers?" These are valid concerns, but he has never tried! Taking a risk to pursue a solution can be stressful. Ironically, settling for less does not seem to make life any less stressful.

I remember working with an 18-year-old guy named Sid. He was always respectful to me in the office. Sid talked a great game. He told me his plans to finish high school, join the Marines, get his driver's license, and move out of his grandmother's house. The grandmother referred him to counseling because "He is not living up to his potential." She was right. Sid had admirable plans, but his lifestyle choices created the opposite outcome. He was already on probation for bringing a knife to school, but he did not seem to care. Sid would promise to follow the rules with reasonable requests like keeping his room clean, staying drug-free, and coming home at curfew. Instead, he would trash his room, come home late, and do all sorts of disrespectful things. He would have one good week and then several bad weeks. Then Sid would try to renegotiate the terms or blame his grandmother for being too uptight. Confusing? Yes. Besides frustrating his grandmother, he was ultimately hurting himself. He was still stuck living at home, extending probation, and moving further away from his goals. Sid proudly stated,

"I am my own man. No one tells me what to do." Is he living an authentic life? My definition of authenticity is similar to integrity. It is when your inside reality matches your outside reality. In other words, what you say you want and how you are living match. If you find that is not the case, the next question to ask yourself is: why does it not match?

Sid's story offers us an answer to that question: it is an illustration of competing commitments. I believe all people are committed. Why do I say that? Because people are following through with decisions every day; everything we do is based on some form of choice and decision-making. But the real question is: are you being committed to your *verbalized* commitments? Being a poor decision maker, the answer is usually no. Let us say that you are constantly late. You want to get to work at 8:00 a.m., but somehow you often get there closer to 8:30 a.m. Yes, there are forces outside of your control like traffic, accidental milk spills, and other deterrents, but the reality is that you are more committed to something else than being on time. The truth is that you do not *really* want to be there at 8:00 a.m. It is not that important. If you truly wanted to be somewhere by 8:00 a.m., you would be there! There is a competing commitment that you are more dedicated to accomplishing. That could be sleeping in that extra 10 minutes. It may be attending to last-minute chores. Or cleaning up that spilled milk. Anything that you "choose" to do instead of getting to work at 8:00 a.m. is your competing commitment. Is it wrong? Not necessarily. Being late may reflect poorly on your reputation and get you fired, but it does not make you a "bad person." The real question is: is being late really your choice? The answer is yes. It may not be your intention, but it is definitely your choice.

Simply put, your decisions can be put into four categories: true choice, false choice, deny choice, and avoid choice. True choice is a decision based on your core values regardless of personal or social consequences. False choice is a decision governed by the opinions of others regarding who you are and how you should behave. Deny choice is a denial of reality and leads to you make decisions based on your own fantasy story. Avoid choice is when you disengage from life and no longer make active decisions. Which mode of decision-making resonates with you most? False choice, deny choice, and avoid choice hinder you from authentic living. The Framework is geared toward helping you choose better. Optimal decision makers make true choices, but it is not the default. It starts with *wanting* to make true choices.

Many people believe that making false choices or avoid choices are easier than making true choices. They think it is easier to go with the flow and not stand up for what they want—or even *identify* what they want—than it is to fight for an authentic life. But to do that can lead to deep-seated unfulfillment with terrible consequences. In a moment of despair, suicidal thoughts make sense to me. Do not get me wrong, I do not believe suicide is the answer. In fact, it is probably the worst decision anyone can make. But when people are in a constant state of lack and inauthenticity, suicide begins to feel tempting. I have sat in a room listening to countless stories of people struggling with suicidal thoughts. Although there are as many reasons as there are people, the general theme is the same. The root of suicide, in many cases, is hopelessness. It is the deep feeling and belief that nothing is ever going to change. People who have suicidal thoughts often do not want to die. The prospect of death freaks them out! Many of them know that their decision to die is selfish and hurtful to their loved ones, yet none of those things seem to matter because their existence is overwhelmingly terrible. It pains them to exist. Their life is filled with guilt, shame, and remorse. Emptiness and sadness poison their everyday experiences. Life does not seem worth living if it continues this way. They no longer want to suffer. Death promises an end to their current existence. When life does not matter to either yourself or other people, why be here anymore? That is the high cost of inauthentic decisions. It leaves people inauthentic and disempowered. How do we break out of this conundrum of simply existing? Live from authenticity by making true decisions that lead to a fulfilling life. That requires getting to know the real you and living congruently before it is too late.

CONCLUSION

We all want to live our lives well; to do that, we must discover who we are and live fully. There are people who have not managed to do this, and who live with strong regrets as they lie on their deathbed. Remember, whether you simply exist or live fully, we will all die one day; everybody dies, but not everybody truly lives. Bronnie Ware, a palliative nurse, wrote a book titled *The Top Five Regrets of the Dying—A Life Transformed by the Dearly Departing* that captures her experiences with her patients who shared their stories during their last moments. She discovered the five most agonizing regrets of the dying:

1. **"I wish I'd had the courage to live a life true to myself, not the life others expected of me."** Many people acknowledged that their various dreams never got fulfilled and were probably never even attempted. They realized that fear or busyness dictated their decisions, such that they neglected

their dreams until it was too late (when their
health began deteriorating).

2. **"I wish I hadn't worked so hard."** Every male
    patient from Ware's research had this regret.
    The older generation of men were the sole
    breadwinners, and work became their dominant
    identity at the cost of time with their kids and
    partners. They worked hard to make as much
    money as possible instead of scaling back to enjoy
    the money with their families.

3. **"I wish I'd had the courage to express my
    feelings."** People often suppressed their
    "inappropriate" feelings to maintain the peace.
    This led to a life of mediocrity and failure to show
    up in an authentic way. These suppressed feelings
    often led to bitterness and resentment. Their
    lack of communication kept other people in the
    dark and they never felt seen. What could have
    happened became a list of regrets.

4. **"I wish I had stayed in touch with my friends."**
    In the busyness of life, we can get overly
    focused on our goals and forget to maintain
    important relationships. When these people

were confronting their own death, it was difficult to locate their friends, and they spent their remaining moments without their loved ones. In the end, they finished life alone.

5. **"I wish that I had let myself be happier."** Happiness is a choice that is often right in front of us. Many people do not give themselves permission to be happy until something "worthy" is accomplished. Or they get accustomed to their old habits to the extent that they deceive themselves into believing "This is as good as it gets." Neither are true. People forget to laugh and be silly because happiness is always a future prospect.[30]

Whoa. Take a moment to let these regrets sink into your consciousness. How many of these regrets resonate with you? The real question is: do you want to live a life without these regrets? Yes, please. Wisdom is benefiting from the lessons of other people's mistakes instead of learning these lessons the hard way. Too many people learn from pain when they could be learning from

---

30   Ware, B. (2019). *The top five regrets of the dying: A life transformed by the dearly departing.* Hay House.

wisdom. By the time these patients realized these truths of inauthentic living, it was already too late. The great news is that these regrets do not have to be yours! It is not too late for you. Your everyday decisions can determine who you are becoming and the trajectory of your life. You can learn the skills to make authentic and optimal choices through a streamlined process called "the Framework."

CHAPTER 4

Cover Your Bases: The Framework

What do pilots and surgeons have in common? They are both highly skilled professionals and yet they are both expected to follow simple protocols before they can do their jobs. Pilots are mandated by the Federal Aviation Administration (FAA) to run through a written "before-takeoff" and "before-landing" checklist, while surgeons must check through a list of tasks to ensure they are ready for surgery, including washing their hands.

This may seem strange. After all, many pilots and surgeons have been doing their jobs for decades. With the advent of technology, the planes practically fly themselves! The "before-takeoff" and "before-landing" checklist includes seemingly obvious items, such as making sure the radio works, seat belts are fastened, and the parking brake is off. Yet history shows appalling accidents occur when pilots ignore this flight safety tool.[31] Similarly, research from the Center for Disease Control and Prevention (CDC) found that healthcare providers wash their hands less than 50% of the time—they need a checklist to remind them. Clean hands are crucial for a good patient survival rate. In 1847, Dr. Ignaz Semmelweis discovered the high mortality rate of mothers giving birth was caused by doctors not washing their hands and transmitting bacteria that led to puerperal fever. When the doctors were required to clean their hands properly, the death rate dropped from 20% to 1%.[32]

So why do knowledgeable professionals need these seemingly simple reminders? Familiarity breeds contempt. It is their familiarity with their job that creates simple errors, sometimes costing other people their lives.

---

31   Butcher, R. (n.d.). Before takeoff checklist: Understanding the benefits of segmented checklists. https://www.aopa.org/training-and-safety/students/presolo/skills/before-takeoff-checklist.

32   Boyce, J. M., & Pittet, D. (2002). Guideline for hand hygiene in healthcare settings: Recommendations of the healthcare infection control practices advisory committee and the HICPAC/SHEA/APIC/IDSA hand hygiene task force. https://www.cdc.gov/mmwr/preview/mmwrhtml/rr5116a1.htm

If such smart people need checklists to guarantee success in their respective fields, why should we be exempt? Somehow, we are above protocols and our autopilot mindset will miraculously make the right decisions? That is delusional. Lazy thinking leads to lazy living. We too need to slow down and double-check our thinking before making our next move. Perhaps you will make the right calls the majority of the time without a checklist, like pilots! After all, they complete the majority of their flights. But can they afford to crash once? Ask yourself: "How many bad decisions can I afford to make?" For there is a high chance that you have already made some poor decisions that cost you much more than you were willing to pay.

Welcome to the Framework! The Framework is critical thinking with heart. Take five and pause. It is stopping at five checkpoints before making any important decision. It provides a systematic way to gain clarity on the problem before determining a solution. With the Framework, you will develop a plan to get unstuck using concrete steps to help inform your final decision.

At first, using the Framework may feel like a time waster. You may be thinking: "Five steps? Who has the time for that?" Remember, though, that the alternative is making poor choices that will cost you even more time and energy. Always take the time upfront to make a *good* decision rather than *carpe diem* and suffer the consequences. Using the Framework is a life skill. Like any skill—nunchuck skills, bow-hunting skills, computer-hacking skills—practice is required to improve. When a coach teaches you how to shoot a basketball, knowing *how* to shoot and actually *making* the basket are two different things. No one is expecting you to execute a skill perfectly after learning it. If this Framework process feels clunky and unnatural...good! That means you are learning a new skill and growing. Keep practicing. The aim is to experience the Framework as a natural way to make decisions. Over time, the Framework will become second nature, like a knee-jerk reaction! You may move away from my original questions and automatically evaluate decisions based on the Framework principles. The Framework training will formulate good cognitive habits.

A common myth is that you *must* make a split-second decision when a problem or challenge arises. Yes, there are situations where immediate action is critical, but the majority of our decisions can wait. Pause. Count to 10... slowly. That pause can be the difference between a good or bad decision. Treat the Framework like a fire drill. (Hopefully you have some experience with a fire drill from school or the workplace.) When a fire alarm goes off, kids are expected to get out of their seats *calmly* and get into a single-file line. They walk to a predetermined area in the field that has been marked out for their class. Then the teacher does a roll call to make sure everyone in that class is accounted for. Why do we have fire drills? To prevent panic and chaos when there is a real fire, which could lead to injury and even death. A time of panic is not the moment to get creative and problem solve; people's survival instincts activate, and poor decisions are mindlessly made. A fire drill is aimed at taking unnecessary thinking out of the decision-making process. The focus is to help people stick to what is important. The Framework is aimed at doing the exact same thing. When circumstances seem to demand an answer when you are under stress and pressure, the Framework helps you focus on a series of important questions to identify your optimal decision.

The United States Army also does something similar when communicating information. It is called the SITREP.[33] SITREP is an abbreviation for SITuation REPort. As a former soldier, I gave brief reports to my commanding officer on our combat status. The SITREP was a mutually understood report that helped colleagues get on the same page without missing any essential details. The

---

33 *Field Manual* No. 6-99.2. (2007). US Army report and message formats. https://usacac.army.mil/sites/default/files/misc/doctrine/CDG/cdg_resources/manuals/fm/fm6_99x2.pdf

report was streamlined, efficient, and crucial for the mission. Each of the 16 lines contained a category of information essential for the leadership to make the most advantageous decisions. For example, Line 1 is the Date and Time, Line 2 is the Unit making the report, Line 12 is the Situation Overview, etc. The Framework is essentially a SITREP for your brain. It cuts out the unnecessary noise and focuses your mind on the important information. Simply put, the Framework outlines the context of the situation so your decisions are well informed. Without identifying the context, it is highly unlikely that a broad answer will resolve the problem.

Now that it is clear why we need the Framework, let us dive into its components. There are five checkpoints in the Framework: Emotion, Values of Self, Values of Others, Reality, and Courage. We will explore the Framework in detail in the next few chapters: chapters 5, 6, 7, 8, and 10 will cover one checkpoint each, while chapter 9 will explain how they all come together in an implemented Framework. But before we dive into the details, I want to provide an overview of these checkpoints so you have a big-picture view of the model.

1. **Emotion: How do I feel and why do I feel this way?** Feelings tend to be the first information we experience when something matters to us.

The emotions are signaling "Pay attention!" to an unmet need or desire. Oftentimes, people are told to ignore "inappropriate" feelings. The funny thing about ignored feelings is that they do not go away. These suppressed emotions will find a way to get your attention, one way or another. Intense emotions then often show up at inconvenient moments that lead to poor decisions. The reason behind the emotions may not always be obvious, which is why the Framework tackles this information first. But remember that emotions are only one portion of the puzzle. People often feel something and then respond immediately, but this leads to poor decisions. You should not base your choices only on emotion. It is like determining the whole picture of a 1,000-piece puzzle from a few pieces. "Oh, I got three blue pieces that connect together. This must be a picture of the ocean with sea animals and mermaids." Well, it may be an aquatic scene but it could also be the sky, a blue T-shirt, a Smurf—anything. Do not let your emotions give you an incomplete picture of the issue.

2. **Values of Self: What is important to me?** The values of self question is about identity. Who are

you and why does this matter? By uncovering more of who you are and what matters to you, you can save a lot of time regarding good decision-making. Unless you are a completely different person every day of the week, your values are going to stay relatively the same. Our values may change over time when exposed to new experiences, but they are generally stable despite varying circumstances. Values are the anchor or north star of authentic living. Optimal decisions are aligned with your values. When you make decisions that are contrary to your values, that is when your emotions begin signaling resentment, hopelessness, and frustration. It may take some time to be honest with yourself and identify your morals. This is the best investment you can make for yourself. Then there are situations when there are conflicting personal values and you cannot choose both. This is when the Values of Others and the Reality factors play a vital role.

3. **Values of Others: What is important to the people involved?** What is important to you may not necessarily be important to others. Good decisions often require "theory of mind." Theory of mind is the ability to understand that people

have their own unique perspectives that may
or may not be the same as your own outlook.[34]
Young children do not understand that people
may not share the same thoughts and feelings as
them, and thus, childish thinking lacks theory
of mind. People have their own thoughts and
feelings. Sometimes, we are fortunate when
all the people involved want the same thing
(which requires communication), so naturally
the decision is agreeable to everyone (which is
ideal). Potential conflict ensues when that is not
the case, especially if the Values of Others are
opposed to the Values of Self. It is important
to identify and consider what matters to other
people in order to work together. We neither want
unnecessary opposition against your Values of
Self nor decisions that hurt the Values of Others.
By doing the challenging work of pinpointing
your Values of Self, you create a foundation to
understand the Values of Others in a similar
situation by priming your mind to more universal
needs and wants.

34   Thompson, B. (2017). Theory of mind: Understanding others in
     a social world. *Psychology Today*. https://www.psychologytoday.
     com/us/blog/socioemotional-success/201707/theory-mind-
     understanding-others-in-social-world

4. **Reality: What are the facts of this situation?**
   Objectivity exists despite how anyone feels about
   a situation. I do not care if you do not believe
   in gravity. When you jump off a flying airplane
   without equipment, you will most likely die.
   These realities have very little to do with what you
   think. These are facts. This is knowledge based
   on our five human senses (touch, sight, hearing,
   smell, and taste). Reality can also be referred to as
   environmental or cultural factors. These variables
   are simply a part of our world and they are not up
   for debate. Reality factors are essentially shared
   "truths" that ground us in our current timeline.
   Choosing to ignore such factors will often leave
   people shocked, frustrated, and disappointed
   when outcomes do not transpire as planned.
   This question honors the "what is" and keeps us
   informed about our decisions.

5. **Courage: Be tough and follow through.** Working
   through the previous four checkpoints allows
   you to make an informed decision. Having the
   optimal answer, however, does not guarantee
   that you will implement the solution. There
   are opposing forces that may cause resistance.
   Understanding the reasons for the resistance will

help you find ways to overcome those challenges and follow through with the optimal decision.

CONCLUSION

Be kind and patient with yourself as you work through the Framework. Answering these questions may be very challenging for you. It may be the first time you have ever sat down and evaluated your emotions or values. Traumatic events or attacks against your identity may have muddled your sense of self. The Framework will provide the essential questions, but you may not uncover certain answers on your own. When you are really stuck, consider seeking professional counseling to navigate these questions together. There is no shame in asking for help if it is going to save you months or years of confusion and pain. Theodore Roosevelt asserted, "Nothing in the world is worth having or worth doing unless it means effort, pain, difficulty...I have never in my life envied a human being who led an easy life. I have envied a great many people who led difficult lives and led them well." Your current life and destiny are worthy endeavors to struggle and fight for.

We will cover each of these checkpoints in greater detail to understand the questions in their entirety. Arriving at the right answer starts with asking the right questions. These are your guideline questions that will get your mind thinking in the right direction. The Framework teaches you to gather important information at your disposal before zeroing in on your final answer. Ready to make optimal decisions and change the course of your life? Let us begin!

CHAPTER 5

Emotions: What Are Your Feelings Telling You?

magine sitting in your car. You are staring at a light on the dashboard that most people dread—the check engine light. People dread this signal because it tells them that something may be wrong with the engine, which translates into major money. Now imagine putting a happy face sticker over the engine light because you do not want to see it. Problem solved, right? But none of us would do that. Why? Because the engine light is not the problem. The actual problem is under the hood of your car. Ignoring the problem now will only cause bigger and more costly problems later. As much as we dislike the light, we are also thankful for the warning.

Your emotions are like the engine light in your car. They exist to try and tell you something important. If we understand this about our car, why do we ignore our feelings? People often treat uncomfortable feelings like a nuisance that makes their lives more difficult. But feelings are your friends; do not ignore your feelings! Avoidance or denial of your emotions will only make matters worse. We must learn to listen to our emotions and ask the important question: "What are my emotions telling me?"

Before we decipher the meaning behind our emotions, it is important to examine emotions themselves. Why do emotions exist? Our emotions are essential to our survival. Neurologist Antonio R. Damasio argued that feelings are crucial for life preservation and play a huge role in our decision-making process and self-image. He made a distinction between emotions and feelings. Emotions are the complex bodily reactions that occur when interacting with a stimulus (e.g., racing heartbeat, sweaty palms), while feelings are the interpretation of those physical sensations in our conscious mind.[35] For our purposes in this book, we will use emotions and feelings interchangeably to capture both experiences.

35   Damasio, A. R. (2004). Emotions and feelings: A neurobiological perspective. In A. S. Manstead (Author), *Feelings and emotions: The Amsterdam Symposium* (49-57). Cambridge Univ. Press.

What are emotions? Psychologist Paul Ekman defined emotions as "a process, a particular kind of automatic appraisal influenced by our evolutionary and personal past, in which we sense that something important to our welfare is occurring, and a set of psychological changes and emotional behaviors begins to deal with the situation."[36] Simply put, emotions provide feedback to your brain that prepares you to respond to important events with little thought. This is particularly true with specific emotions, such as fear or anger, that deliver high-speed feedback in response to potential harm. The limbic system of our brain, which contains the amygdala, activates our fight-or-flight mode to address the perceived threat. How quickly? Dr. Joseph LeDoux, a psychologist at the Center for Neural Science at New York University, reported that our brain receives the signal in 40 milliseconds (or 1/25th of a second). It is challenging to use our rational mind when intense emotions occur because the emotions get to our brain so much faster! The fight-or-flight response increases our chance of survival by propelling adrenaline in our bodies to react in almost superhuman ways. There are many stories of people who were able to

---

36   Ekman, P. (2007). *Emotions revealed: Recognizing faces and feelings to improve communication and emotional life*. St. Martin's Griffin.

perform superhuman acts to free someone from getting crushed. In 2016, 19-year-old Charlotte Heffelmire lifted a GMC truck off her father after he was pinned down when the car jack slipped and then the truck caught on fire. She proceeded to hustle into the burning truck, drove it out of the garage, and got everyone out of the house, including her baby sister.[37] That is the power of our emotions and how it can fuel important action.

I believe emotions have another function besides survival. Feelings allow us to enjoy our life! They add richness and beauty to our experience. Some people believe that life would be much better if we were all robots void of feelings, and it is true that robots would probably make more logical choices, but they would lack originality and creativity. I remember seeing a patient named Monica, who was clinically depressed and had been prescribed antidepressants to stabilize her mood. She told me that the medication was working because her emotions were less labile, but she stopped taking them after a couple of months. When I asked her why, Monica told me, "The medication helped me feel less sad, but I was unable to feel happy as well. In fact, I was not able to feel much of

37 Fox, P. (2016). Teen girl uses 'crazy strength' to lift burning car off dad. *USA Today*. https://www.usatoday.com/story/news/humankind/2016/01/12/teen-girl-uses-crazy-strength-lift-burning-car-off-dad/78675898/

anything at all and I hated it." A life without feelings is like a painting void of color.

I have introduced emotions as the first part of the Framework because our feelings tend to grab our attention the quickest whenever something important occurs. Emotions happen so suddenly! I am a firm believer that you only feel strong emotions toward what is important to you. Otherwise, who cares? Why would you get angry about what does not even matter to you? Or get upset with someone who does not matter to you? If I criticized 16th century US history as being useless information, most people would probably feel little to nothing about it. On the other hand, if I called your mother "stupid and worthless" (assuming you do not hate your mother), you would no longer feel neutral. What you feel matters and why you feel that way matters too.

As an early-career psychologist, I would get annoyed when people would sarcastically ask, "How does that make you feel?" I felt like my profession was being reduced to merely "feelings talk" when therapists do so much more (e.g., provide emotional support, present healthy perspectives, impart psychological insights, educate on various topics). Now that I am a more seasoned psychologist, however, I have realized that emotions matter more than I ever imagined. It genuinely matters how you feel. Why? *Because emotions are connected to a deeper part of who we are and reveal our values.* Our feelings can provide important clues about our identity and surface values that are at times beyond our awareness.

SEVEN PRIMARY EMOTIONS

Talking about our emotions is only the beginning. We need to learn how to identify what we feel and why we feel this way. But what do my emotions mean? Dr. Paul Ekman, the leading expert on emotions, identified seven universal emotions that exist across cultures. I want to further break down some of our primary emotions, what they mean and signal, common expressions of that emotion, the range of intensity for that emotion from least to greatest (when applicable), and a good question to ask yourself when you feel it.

Anger

Anger is an emotion that tends to flare up when there is a sense that something is unfair or wrong.[38] It provides us with the strength to fight injustice. Along the same lines, anger can also present itself to protect us from feeling vulnerable. It is important to note that just because

---

38 Ekman, P. (n.d.). Anger. https://www.paulekman.com/universal-emotions/what-is-anger/

something *feels* wrong does not necessarily mean something *is* wrong. Anger is an emotion that signals something feels off, so it is often wise to talk and think through issues before acting. Common expressions of anger include yelling, aggressive behaviors, feeling hot, muscle tension, clenching jaw and/or fists, rapid heart rate, puffing up one's chest to appear bigger, eyes widening, furrowed eyebrows, and tightly pressed lips. The range of anger (from least to greatest intensity) includes annoyance, frustration, exasperation, argumentativeness, bitterness, vengefulness, and fury. A good question to ask yourself or an angry somebody is **"What feels unfair or wrong?"**

Sadness

Sadness seeps into our heart when we have lost something valuable.[39] On a deeper level, sadness is experienced when our desired expectations for something, someone, or even ourselves fall short. People often feel sad about being rejected by someone important, losing a loved one, having to say goodbye, losing an ability to do something, and disappointment from an undesired outcome. On a deeper level, sadness may be generated from a lack of valuable goals or the inability to reach them.

---

39 Ekman, P. (n.d.). Sadness. https://www.paulekman.com/
universal-emotions/what-is-sadness/

Oftentimes, sadness signals comfort and support to ease our heartache. Common expressions of sadness include tightness in the chest, pressure in the heart and stomach area, heaviness in the body, watery eyes, numbness, looking away or downward, being hunched over, crying, eyes drooped downward, and lip corners being pulled downward. The range of sadness (from least to greatest intensity) includes disappointment, discouragement, distraughtness, resignation, helplessness, hopelessness, misery, despair, grief, sorrow, and anguish. A good question to ask yourself or someone is **"What has been lost or what do I feel is missing?"**

Happiness/Joy

This is the emotion that most people want or strive for because joy is an indicator of satisfaction and well-being.[40] Psychologist Jordan Peterson framed happiness as an emotion that gets signaled when our minds are able to see an open pathway toward obtaining something valuable.[41] The more valuable the goal, the greater the

---

40   Ekman, P. (n.d.). Enjoyment. https://www.paulekman.com/universal-emotions/what-is-enjoyment/

41   Peterson, J. (n.d.). Life's never just about happiness—it's about meaning. *The Australian.* https://www.theaustralian.com.au/commentary/opinion/lifes-never-just-about-happiness-its-about-meaning/news-story/b8f6d4beb93d1e2173114e40b7cca423

happiness! The difference between happiness and joy is that happiness tends to be a by-product of obtaining the desired outcome, while joy is a more stable feeling of contentment that resides in a deeper part of us. Joy signals that things are good! Common expressions of happiness include feeling upbeat, energetic, warm, relaxed, grounded, laughter, contentment, eyes narrowed with wrinkles on the side (known as crow's feet), and smiling. The range of happiness (from least to most intense) includes sensory pleasure, rejoicing, compassion, amusement, schadenfreude, relief, peace, pride, fiero, naches, wonder, excitement, and ecstasy. Good questions to ask yourself or someone else is **"What are you grateful for?"** or **"What do you want to celebrate?"**

Fear/Anxiety

I have grouped fear and anxiety together because both feelings have a survival function but differ in their sources. Fear is conjured up when we sense danger either physically, emotionally, and/or socially.[42] Anxiety is a nervousness and often is a worry about potential harm. These feelings can signal a fight-flight-freeze-faint reaction to avoid harm or an overpowering threat. People often experience

---

42   Ekman, P. (n.d.). Fear. https://www.paulekman.com/universal-emotions/what-is-fear/

fear around dangerous animals, heights, darkness, and death. Anxiety is often experienced around uncertainty of the future, imaginable humiliation, probable rejection, and other pending threats. Common expressions of fear include increased heart palpitations, shortness of breath, trembling, higher pitched voice, freezing posture, raised eyebrows, and lowering of the jaw. The range of fear (from least to most intense) includes trepidation, nervousness, anxiety, dread, desperation, panic, horror, and terror. A good question to ask yourself or someone else is **"What threat is making you feel unsafe or worry about future harm?"**

Surprise

This emotion can be experienced as an interesting mixture of fear and delight. Surprise begins as fear until the brain interprets the source as either being positive or harmful.[43] Surprise also pushes us into a fight-or-flight mode to attend to the unexamined situation. It creates a startle response to halt our current actions for a few seconds and directs our attention to the new situation. We may feel embarrassed and/or pleased when something wonderful gets revealed. Or we may undergo misery from

---

43   Ekman, P. (n.d.). Surprise. https://www.paulekman.com/universal-emotions/what-is-surprise/

a negative outcome, leading to disappointment or devastation. People tend to feel surprised when they experience loud sounds or unexpected movements. Common expressions of surprise include attentiveness, gasping, and moving into a defensive posture. Common questions may be **"What information did I miss to be caught off guard?"** or **"Is this surprise helpful or harmful to me?"**

Disgust

Disgust may feel like a hybrid between anger and anxiety, but it is a distinct emotion. The feeling of disgust occurs when we experience something that may cause sickness and therefore needs to be rejected.[44] This is most commonly felt with poisonous or bad food. We could also feel disgust when someone does something morally wrong. People often feel disgusted with ugliness, rotting or diseased entities, unappealing foods, expelled bodily fluids like vomit and blood, and behavioral perversion like torture. There are also culturally determined constructs that have communicated certain people or things as being "bad," even if that is not objectively true (e.g., racism, sexism, lower hierarchical status), which will be further examined in chapter 8. Common expressions of

---

44   Ekman, P. (n.d.). Disgust. https://www.paulekman.com/
     universal-emotions/what-is-disgust/

disgust include nausea, vomiting, gagging, turning away from the source, covering one's mouth or nose, making sounds like "ew," and wrinkling one's nose. The range of disgust (from least to the most intense) includes dislike, aversion, distaste, repugnance, revulsion, abhorrence, and loathing. A good question to ask is **"What factors are causing me to feel disgusted and why?"**

Contempt

This is a feeling of superiority over another person, group, or actions through negative judgment.[45] It has a combination of "I am better than you" and "you are lesser than me." The purpose of contempt is to assert power or status. We feel more powerful and distinguished as being someone with authority. Although some people derive pleasure from feeling superior, others may feel embarrassed or shameful for such arrogant feelings. Common expressions of contempt include smugness, a disapproving tone of voice, tension, feeling powered up, rolling one's eyes, looking "down your nose," and raising one corner of your mouth. A good question to ask when contempt arises may be **"Why do I feel the need to be better than someone else?"**

---

45   Ekman, P. (n.d.). Contempt. https://www.paulekman.com/
       universal-emotions/what-is-contempt/

Emotions occur for a purpose. Hopefully, the summaries above have offered you a better understanding of your emotions and where they come from. As you may already know, emotions can be complicated. After all, humans are complex beings. Professor W. Gerrod Parrott (2001) created a chart based on his Theory of Emotions that breaks down the seven primary emotions into nuanced secondary and tertiary emotions under their respective subcategories.[46] If you want to advance your emotional intelligence, strive to describe your feelings beyond the primary seven emotions. The secondary and tertiary emotions give voice to the varying quality and intensity of your emotions, which informs your why. Often, we have multiple emotions happening at once; indeed, it is pretty rare to feel only a single emotion, such as sadness, and nothing else. There are confusing emotions like jealousy, which stems from the threat of losing something or someone valuable to a rival and yet contains other intense emotions like love, anger, powerlessness, and disgust. Often, there is a blend of simultaneous emotions like 35% sadness, 25% anger, and 40% fear. You do not need to identify the percentages of your emotions, but you should recognize that multiple emotions are all telling you something important.

---

46 Parrott, W. G. (Ed.). (2001). *Emotions in social psychology: Essential readings*. Psychology Press.

Identifying your emotions is a crucial first step, and it varies in difficulty depending on your upbringing. It seems like in many cultures, men are only allowed two masculine emotions: anger and happiness (but not too happy!). Women are only allowed two feminine emotions: sadness and happiness. If your family or the people around you modeled only certain emotions, then it can be really challenging to identify and comprehend other emotions. There are no masculine or feminine emotions (though literature may categorize feelings as such). There are simply human emotions. If you are a healthy human being, you will feel the whole spectrum of emotions. There are also psychological defenses that may block certain feelings from awareness because these emotional experiences have been hurtful in the past. People have therefore learned to suppress them out of fear of negative consequences. Those suppressed feelings are still there, and may lead to other unpleasant manifestations. For example, people experience physical pain from holding in unattended feelings. Other people unconsciously harm themselves or others in a futile attempt to work through their feelings. The common conclusion in the scientific community is that up to 90% of our decisions are driven by emotions. Ninety percent! Without proper awareness of our feelings, we may act in contrary ways against our better judgment. George

Loewenstein, psychologist and economist at Carnegie Mellon University, identified the hot-cold empathy gap as people's tendency to underestimate the influence of emotions over their actions. When emotions are dormant or "cold," people are able to think and act rationally. When emotions are aroused and "hot," people can make uncharacteristic decisions that lead to regrettable consequences.[47] This means that people can think and act in surprising ways when they are hungry, afraid, or in pain. It is not just knowing yourself under calm conditions, but also knowing who you are in all emotional states. The ability to properly address your feelings will largely dictate the extent of your well-being.

Increasing your emotional vocabulary and understanding will help you master the Framework. This is also known as emotional intelligence. Salovey, Mayer, and Caruso (2008) defined emotional intelligence as "the ability to engage in sophisticated information processing about one's own and others' emotions and the ability to use this information as a guide to thinking and behavior. That is, individuals high in emotional intelligence pay attention to, use, understand, and manage emotions, and these skills serve adaptive functions that potentially

47 Loewenstein, G. (2005). Hot-cold empathy gaps and medical decision-making. *Health Psychology*, 24(Suppl. 4), S49-S56.

benefit themselves and others."[48] Psychologist Daniel Goleman identified the main components of emotional intelligence as self-awareness, self-regulation, internal motivation, empathy, and social skills. Self-awareness is the ability to identify and articulate your thoughts and feelings, especially when they are happening in real time. Self-regulation is the ability to manage the expression of your thoughts and feelings in a professional way, especially when emotions are felt intensely. Internal motivation is having the drive to live out your values. Empathy is the ability to understand, communicate, and sense how other people think and feel. Social skills are verbal and nonverbal actions that connect, build, and maintain healthy relationships.[49] The Framework aims to polish and refine all of these components of emotional intelligence as you holistically consider all the crucial information before making a decision. Increasing your ability to make optimal decisions will naturally strengthen your emotional intelligence as well!

Emotions may indicate whether something is important, but they will not tell you *why*. Think of emotions as

---

48   Mayer, J. D., Salovey, P. S., & Caruso, D. R. (2008, September). Emotional intelligence: New ability or eclectic traits. *American Psychologist*, 63(6), 503–517.

49   Goleman, D. (2000). *Working with emotional intelligence*. Bantam Books.

a smoke detector. A smoke detector does one thing well: it lets you know that there is smoke in a certain area. Smoke detectors do not tell you the kind of fire, the cause of the smoke, or any other information. It just sets off the alarm! In the same way, our emotions tell us to pay attention, but we need to figure out what those feelings are trying to say.

That is why we need to pause and think about our emotions. If not, we may misinterpret the reason for the emotion and make a poor decision based on the wrong information. This often occurs when people make poor choices. For example, I may feel irritated when my wife criticizes how I do chores. Usually, I let the feeling lie and do not say anything. This particular day, however, I yell at her with intense anger when she points out a dirty dish. The reaction is grossly out of proportion to the offense. When I take a little time to process my anger, I realize my deeper frustration is about my coworker criticizing my work all week. I felt incompetent at work and my wife's comment about the dishes thus triggered my insecurities. The angry outburst was my unconscious way of defending myself and protesting. My lack of insight and unprocessed feelings led me to mistreat my wife and cause her pain. When our emotions are left unchecked, we end up causing regrettable outcomes.

FEELING FACTS

Feeling Fact #1

We do not choose our emotions. Our emotions choose us! Feelings happen quicker than our consciousness. They are automatic responses to our thoughts, somatic feelings, and other external information. That is why it is unfair to blame people for how they feel. People do not get to *pick* their feelings. Shaming yourself or another person for their feelings will not make them stop. The person may suppress or hide their feelings, but the feelings themselves do not go away. And oftentimes, the suppression of strong emotions ends up fueling the problem! The only path forward is to acknowledge the feelings and make space for them with compassion.

Feeling Fact #2

There are no right or wrong feelings. Emotions may be more or less enjoyable, but they are neither good nor evil. Feelings are simply feelings. We have a tendency to categorize our emotions. Anger, sadness, fear, contempt, and disgust are grouped as "bad" feelings, which only leaves happy as a "good" feeling. No wonder people avoid feelings—the majority of our emotions are demonized! This is like saying money is either good or bad. Money is *neutral*. It is just a tool that our society uses to make the exchange of goods easier. Money can be exploited for evil purposes, like bribing judges for unfair rulings, purchasing illegal weapons, or influencing people in a negative way. That same money can also be utilized for good purposes, like providing medicine for the sick, building schools, and providing clean water. Just like money can be used for good or evil, our feelings can be catalysts for good or evil behaviors. The feelings themselves are not good or bad; it is what we do with those feelings that determines their morality.

Feeling Fact #3

Feelings indicate needs. Abraham Maslow is a psychologist who developed his famous Maslow's hierarchy of needs. The theory is that humans have five levels of needs, but we cannot attend to the higher-level needs until we meet the lower level ones first. On the most bottom tier, we have physiological needs such as water, food, warmth, and rest. The next level is our safety needs, which include protection, security, and shelter. When our basic needs are met, then we can begin addressing our psychological needs. The next level is the need to belong and love, which includes intimate relationships, friends, colleagues, and community. Then we move to our esteem needs, which are our desire for mastery, identity, and accomplishment.[50] When our basic and psychological needs are met, we eventually reach "self-actualization" or being your fully authentic self. Being your authentic self encompasses a life with purpose and calling. The Maslow hierarchy concept allows you to ask yourself, "Is there an unmet need? If so, on which level?" When people get "hangry" or hungry-angry, being able to address relational needs becomes exponentially more difficult! The anger may seem directed toward the colleague who keeps asking "stupid questions," but really you are just hungry. Accurately identifying the need will help shift your emotions and behaviors accordingly.

Daniel Pink, the author of *Drive: The Surprising Truth About What Motivates Us*, emphasizes the human needs for autonomy, mastery, and purpose.[51] From the perspective of Maslow's hierarchy of needs, these three motivations are specific aspects of our esteem needs. Autonomy is being our own person—someone who takes ownership of his or her decisions and engagement. Mastery is the desire to be good at different skills, which increases our competency. And, lastly, purpose is the desire for our decisions and activities to be

---

50 McLeod, S. (2020). *Maslow's hierarchy of needs*. Simply Psychology. https://www.simplypsychology.org/maslow.html

51 Pink, D. H. (2009). *Drive: the Surprising truth about what motivates us*. Riverhead Books.

meaningful. Are your feelings indicating one of these drives are being unfulfilled?

CONCLUSION

What if you have no clue how you feel? When in doubt, ask someone you trust! Tell them your situation and ask how they would feel. Then ask the person *why* he or she would feel that way. See if anything the person is sharing makes sense to you. Do the feelings match with some of the universal feelings we previously discussed? Can you identify with the underlying message behind the emotion? Talking about your feelings gives you a set of working ideas; it allows you to have a starting point. Given that we are not all-knowing, we must formulate different theories to see which one resonates with us the most. Over time, you will learn to be more attuned with your feelings and why you feel that way, which provides essential information to your decision-making equation.

Our emotions indicate important needs that should not be ignored. These needs are strongly linked to our beliefs and values. In fact, our feelings would only linger for a short time if they were not interconnected to particular thoughts! Dr. Jill Bolte Taylor, a Harvard-trained neuroscientist, noted that the physiological response to your emotions (e.g., racing heartbeat, muscle tension) only lasts about 90 seconds.[52] When is the last time your feelings continued for such a brief period? Rarely. With more intense emotions, the feelings may last for hours or even days! So, what keeps our emotions going for so long? It is our thoughts and the stories we keep telling ourselves about the situation. Thoughts are where our emotions derive meaning. We must gain clarity on our cognitions in order to decrypt our emotions more accurately. The second factor for optimal decision-making, therefore, is identifying our values and beliefs.

52   Bolte Taylor, J. (2016). *My stroke of insight: A brain scientist's personal journey.* Plume.

CHAPTER 6

Values of Self: What Matters to Me?

"I couldn't see through my glasses, Drill Sergeant," I said. There was a moment's pause. Then the drill sergeant punched me in the stomach. The hit was so hard, it knocked the wind out of me. I doubled over and then fell to the ground; I could not breathe. I looked up desperately for help, and my eyes met the senior drill sergeant's standing next to me. He scoffed and laughed. The drill sergeant who punched me said, "I hate whiners. Now get out of my face, Ying Yang."

This was my moment of despair during my US Army boot camp. I was unable to see through the humidity that formed on my glasses due to the Georgia summer heat and could not accurately shoot my rifle for qualification.

Instead of getting support from my leaders, I experienced physical assault, humiliation, and racist remarks. Then I reminded myself that no one forced me to join the army; I volunteered *against* the wishes of my mom. I wanted to earn the GI Bill so the government would pay for my college tuition, which would alleviate the financial burden on my parents. I valued personal growth, career training, and adventure. So, while that incident with the glasses and the drill sergeant was tough, one thing helped me get through this dark time: my values. I knew my identity and my purpose for being there.

WHO ARE YOU, REALLY?

Based on her research with thousands of people from all over the world, organizational psychologist Tasha Eurich stated, "Even though most people believe they are self-aware, only 10–15% of the people we studied actually fit the criteria."[53] There is a high probability that you may be less self-aware than you realize! Who are you? No, really. Who are you, really? Many people live their lives never asking themselves this important question. Without proper

---

53   Eurich, T. (2018). What self-awareness really is (and how to cultivate it). *Harvard Business Review*. https://hbr.org/2018/01/what-self-awareness-really-is-and-how-to-cultivate-it.

introspection, we may only have surface-level answers to that question. You may automatically think of your roles such as, "I am a husband, a son, or an employee." Or you may associate your identity with your profession, religious background, or ethnicity. These attributes are *aspects* of your identity, but they do not define who you are. We want to discover the deeper parts of your identity that comprise your values and purpose.

Think about a dog. How do dogs know they are dogs? They just do. Dogs simply own their identity. They do not prove their identity by running after a stick, barking, or wagging their tail. Dogs naturally do those behaviors because they are dogs! The behaviors do not define the dog. Dogs define the behavior. In the same way, our identity is not based on performance. We are human beings, not human doings! Just as dogs are more than their mannerisms, a person's worth is not defined by their behaviors. We are much more than our past history or anything that may weigh us down. As an aspiring optimal decision maker, we must start with the notion that we are inherently worthy. We do not prove it. We are innately valuable people; we are inherently precious. We choose to own that truth. We start with the belief that all people are intrinsically significant as an a priori, a working foundation for our other values. As Brené Brown, a professor and author on authentic living, says beautifully, "Worthiness does not have prerequisites. We need to find a way to engage people from a place of worthiness. We need to find a way to say 'I am enough. This is who I am.'"[54]

Your true identity is comprised of your values. Knowing your values allows for authentic living and optimal decision-making. We want to avoid taking a shortcut by simply behaving better. Saying the right words or acting the right way will not address the heart issues of your identity. If you cut off the leaves, the weeds may look like they are gone. But what happens a couple weeks later? The leaves grow back and even begin spreading to different areas. By focusing only on the surface issues like wanting to feel happier, the problem often gets worse and unresolved. We kill the weeds by digging out its roots, not simply trimming the leaves. When we deal with the root of the issue (core needs and wants), the leaves (the symptoms) get resolved as a natural by-product. Yes, sharpening our behavioral interventions are still important, but it should be predicated on the heart of the issue. Address the needs, emotions, and intentions to clarify your values.

In this chapter, we want to better understand the importance of values and define them more specifically.

---

54 Palouse Mindfulness. (2019, April 30). *The Call to Courage—Brené Brown compilation* [Video]. YouTube. https://www.youtube.com/watch?v=zDIQQx1KNZc

Identifying your values is crucial to living an authentic life. After all, how can you be authentic if you do not know what matters to you in life? I will introduce a variety of ways to begin your process of articulating your values that include psychological assessments, existential questions, and activities. I will share a short version of my own values and their basis to give you an example of what it may sound like for you. We will also talk about the kind of legacy you want to leave behind and redefine your decisions based on it.

UNDERSTANDING VALUES

There is a reason why certain things matter more to you than others. For me, people and their stories interest me the most. Humans are the most fascinating subjects! They are predictable and simultaneously unique. I can meet 10 people with depression, yet none of them will share the same combination of reasons for their depression. I naturally gravitate toward people's stories and improving their lives because that is what renders my life more meaningful. When you ask me about math, suddenly my excitement goes to zero. Who cares about calculus? Why do these symbols matter? To a mathematician, I am speaking blasphemy! The math enthusiast could argue why math is the ONLY thing that really matters and makes sense. So why do we draw such different conclusions? Because people are uniquely wired down to their DNA, and we intrinsically care about different things. One of life's greatest adventures is figuring out what truly matters to you in order to live a life of significance.

So, what are values? It is simply what really matters to you; what is truly important. Values are your *why*. It is the reason for your existence. Simon Sinek, author of *Start with Why: How Great Leaders Inspire Everyone to Take Action*, shared this wisdom: "Regardless of WHAT we do in our lives, our WHY—our driving purpose, cause or belief —never changes."[55] Understanding your *why* allows you to align all your decisions, actions, and communications on what is important. Values can be anything from what you find appealing (e.g., the ocean, luxury watches) to the character traits (e.g., loyalty, open-mindedness) of other people. Like we discussed in our chapter on feelings, emotions are heavily linked to your values because feelings indicate importance. You feel strongly toward things that matter. Your individual values act as a compass to guide your way into living an authentic life. When you get clear about your values, then you can evaluate your decisions and behaviors based on that metric. For example,

---

55   Sinek, S. (2019). *Start with why: How great leaders inspire everyone to take action.* Portfolio Penguin.

let us say "love" is one of your top values and you define it as actions that benefit the other person. The next time you are frustrated at your spouse, value-driven decisions would first ask, "Do my words reflect love or not?" There is greater awareness and accountability when you assess your decisions based on identified values. You know when your judgments are on track or starting to detour.

Your personal values are informed by your character traits, as well as your personal morality and ethics. People do not care about all human virtues equally. A person may care about being truthful more than being kind, for instance. Most importantly, though, your values are defined by actions. It is not just what you say; it is what you do. Individuals may say they care about integrity, but their actions speak differently when a questionable financial opportunity presents itself. In that instance, gaining money is the dominant value, not their integrity. Hard truth, huh? Identifying your values is not a cute exercise of listing nice-sounding virtues. Your emotions and actions will uncover what you *really* value. A few verses in the Bible sum up this concept. In Matthew 7:17 and 20, it says, "A good tree produces good fruit, and a bad tree produces bad fruit...Yes, just as you can identify a tree by its fruit, so you can identify people by their actions." Luke 6:45 reads, "A good man brings good things out of the good stored up in his heart, and an evil man brings evil things out of the evil stored up in his heart. For the mouth speaks what the heart is full of." The decisions that we make are a reflection of our values. What do your actions say about your values?

We want to think about identifying your values in a holistic manner. You are a whole person comprised of different expressions. We may think about ourselves as having physical, emotional, mental, and spiritual parts. Although we can conceptualize our personhood in these different aspects, we cannot function without these parts influencing one another. These parts of ourselves work together in unison. When people operate from only their mental rationale while ignoring their emotional side, they begin developing mental and emotional disorders. It is difficult to stay "open-minded" in our mindset when our emotions are sending signals of disgust and fear. We may need to take extra time to reevaluate why there is a disconnect between parts. Each of these personal parts need to be congruent and on the same page. The aim is to live as a whole person. The Framework is geared toward making decisions that are connected to your whole self. I would define health as having all aspects of yourself thriving congruently and harmoniously. It removes the unnecessary commotion in our heads and hearts.

Living according to your values will ultimately contribute to a life that matters to you. As explored in the chapters above, authenticity is an important value for optimal decision-making and a fulfilling life. In contrast, living inauthentically often leads to a fragmented sense of self that causes general distress. Remember that people tend to have a variety of values that are important to them. For example, excitement and novelty may be important to Kelly, and she expresses this by her participation in high-risk sports. On the other hand, she also values safety and security, which is lived out by using excessive protective gear and following strict protocols. Making optimal decisions requires incorporating the right values in the proper situation. Aspiring to live out these values consistently creates a more optimal life.

Viktor Frankl, psychiatrist and author of *Man's Search for Meaning*, summed up meaningful living by saying,

There are three main avenues on which one arrives at meaning in life. The first is by creating a work or doing a deed. The second is by experiencing something or encountering someone; in other words, meaning can be found not only in work but also in love...Most important, however, is the third avenue to meaning in life— even the helpless victim of a hopeless situation, facing a fate he cannot change, may rise above himself, may grow beyond himself, and by so doing change himself. He may turn a personal tragedy into a triumph. Just as life remains potentially meaningful under any conditions, even those which are most miserable, so too does the value of each and every person stay with him or her, and it does so because it is based on the values that he or she has realized in the past, and is not contingent on the usefulness that he or she may or may not remain in the present.[56]

I believe the values that really matter are often aligned with Frankl's meaningful components of work, love, and a cause that transcends our own needs. It is living for a reason that goes beyond one's own happiness and contributes to a greater good.

Next, we will discover ways to engage meaningfully in life by uncovering your values.

FINDING YOUR VALUES

Living well means creating values that are aligned with your individuality. So how do we know our values? There are several ways to begin a dialogue about values. As a starting point, begin by discerning your personal values

---

56   Chachura, R. (2019). *'Man's Search for Meaning' by Viktor E. Frankl.* Medium. https://medium.com/@geekrodion/mans-search-for-meaning-by-viktor-e-frankl-7b71b4693790

and what is most important to you. By identifying your individual values, you establish a universal baseline for your decision-making. Your values become the reference point with which you compare your decisions. For those who are new to identity formation work, figuring out values may require experimentation with different facets of identities and experiences. When the dust settles, acquiring a consistent list of values requires maintenance, as you add more life experiences. "Maintenance" here is defined as revisiting those values and reevaluating them to make sure they are still true for you. People do change and new life experiences can drastically put our old values into question. That is not necessarily a bad thing! The process allows us to get closer to who we really are. Without our identities being tested, we can actually form a false identity and deceive ourselves.

One great way to identify your values is through psychological assessments. After all, a vital part of finding the right answers is asking the right questions. Psychological tests can reveal important information about yourself, and can help organize that information into understandable answers about your values. My personal favorite is the Enneagram personality test. This is a great tool to discover your personality type. It uncovers what makes you tick and why! It also reveals your personality under pressure and reveals the "dark and unhealthy" aspects of yourself. Other great personality tests include the gold standard, Big Five Personality Test (e.g., 16PF, NEO-PI-R, IPIP-NEO), DISC, LIFO Survey, or even the Myers-Briggs Type Indicator (MBTI) for starters. These are great tools to get yourself asking some honest questions. Get to know yourself first! Though these results may not explicitly spell out your values, the answers of these tests will point to your intrinsic strengths and personal qualities. Understanding your personality will then help sort out the characteristics that inform your values.

Disclaimer: You may have the temptation to answer self-report questions favorably rather than honestly. Do not answer the questions based on how you *want* to be, but rather on how you actually think or feel most often. Similarly, do not answer the questions in an overly negative way either. The mindset is to answer these situational questions based on how you would respond "most of the time." Sometimes, the "first thought, best thought" mentality can help minimize overanalyzing your answers.

As a brief example, I will share a small portion of my Enneagram results. My highest score for my personality type was a Type Three. Type Three is also known as the Achiever, whose leading motivation is success and efficiency. It revealed my strong desire for accomplishment and being the best version of myself. This is partially why I am driven to write this book, because the values of being my best and helping others be their best matter to me! Type Three people tend to equate personal worth with performance and positive outward appearances. When I am experiencing immense stress, my restlessness often leads to familiar routines and "busyness" even if my actions are straying away from other core values. My desire to gain positive feedback from others can tempt me to fake a positive façade, which takes away from my authenticity. With these Enneagram results, I became more aware of my strengths and shortcomings. It reminds me to place my worth in more permanent qualities like God's perspective of me, and my values while striving for excellence as its own reward rather than the praise of people. My value in personal growth helps me leverage my strengths while also addressing my shortcomings. What do your personality test results reveal about you?

Then there are specific tests that reveal other aspects of yourself. Hogan's Motive, Values, Preference Inventory (MVPI) identifies your natural affinity toward certain values (e.g., aesthetics, affiliation, altruism, commerce, hedonism, power, recognition, science, security, and tradition). Preferences are neither good nor bad. People are simply wired to care about certain things over others. CliftonStrengths 34 (also known as StrengthsFinder

2.0) by Donald O. Clifton and The StandOut Assessment by Marcus Buckingham highlight your top strengths and provide ideas on how to incorporate them into your life. Emotional Intelligence 2.0 by Travis Bradberry and Jean Greaves utilizes the four domains that comprise emotional intelligence, assesses your ranking in each area, and suggests specific skills to strengthen that domain. [57]*The Speed of Trust* by Stephen Covey also has a short assessment to identify your level of trust (integrity, intent, capabilities, and results) and provides ways to improve areas of weakness.[58] To identify your values within a romantic relationship, consider taking the Prepare/Enrich assessment, which will identify areas of growth

---

57   Psychological Assessments: Enneagram: https://tests. enneagraminstitute.com/orders/create#rheti; 16PF: https:// www.16-personality-types.com/online-personality-tests/16pf-test-online/; NEO-PI-R: https://sapa-project.org/blogs/NEOmodel. html; IPIP-NEO: https://www.personal.psu.edu/~j5j/IPIP/; DISC: https://discpersonalitytesting.com/free-disc-test/; LIFO survey: https://lifo.co/getting-started-lifo-process/lifo-survey/; MBTI: https://www.myersbriggs.org/my-mbti-personality-type/take-the-mbti-instrument/; Hogan's Motive, Values Preference Inventory (MVPI): https://www.hoganassessments.com/assessment/ motives-values-preferences-inventory/; CliftonStrengths 34: https://www.gallup.com/cliftonstrengths/en/252137/home.aspx; The StandOut Assessment: https://www.marcusbuckingham. com; Emotional Intelligence 2.0: https://www.talentsmart.com/ test/; Prepare/Enrich: https://www.prepare-enrich.com

58   Covey, S. M. (2006). *The speed of trust.* Free Press.

and strength across the most important nine domains in a relationship (e.g., communication style, sexual expectations, relationship roles, spiritual beliefs, financial management, partner style and habits, conflict resolution, and family and friends) in relation to your partner's scores. My wife and I utilized the Prepare/Enrich assessment in our premarital counseling and it helped us enter marriage with greater awareness! Rarely did our conflicts surprise us because we were prepared for those issues. Whatever assessments you decide to take, the important thing is to acquire information that helps you discover your identity and values. (For websites and resources on these tests mentioned above, please refer to the reference section.)

If you do not want to take these formal assessments, there are other ways to uncover your values. I have personally experienced more informal methods to gain additional clarity about myself. The Passion Test by Janet and Chris Attwood goes through a series of questions and has you rank your interests from most important to least important. Examples of these questions include:

- "What subject could I read 500 books or watch countless videos about without getting bored?"
- "What would I spend my time doing if I had complete financial abundance to do anything?"

- "If you could do anything knowing you could not fail, what would you do?"[59]

You could also do a modified version by using a list of more generic values for consideration. Before referencing a list of values, consider writing out values from memory first and see what you can identify. Then, simply search for "list of values" on a search engine like Google. There are lists that range from 50 to 200 values. Pick a list (perhaps choose a shorter list for starters). You can add your own values and write them down. Review the list and circle the values that resonate more strongly for you. Your thoughts and feelings play a vital role. When you are comparing each item to see which value ranks higher than another, I would recommend starting with your feelings. Which values provoke a stronger feeling? When you take a moment to marinate with that value in mind, does it induce a weightiness in your heart? Then engage your mind and decipher why those feelings are resonating stronger with certain values. Define what the value means to you. Take time to explain the importance of having that value experienced in your life. Then begin ranking the values in the order of significance. Sit with

---

59 Attwood, J. B., & Attwood, C. (2009). *The passion test: The effortless path to discovering your destiny*. Pocket.

the values on your list and compare them one by one. For example, you may have freedom and family on the list. If you had to choose, which one resonates more strongly? If it is a personal freedom over family, then move personal freedom up the list. Then you can compare family with money and continue down that process. It is important not to judge yourself on whether a value is "right" or "appropriate." Values are just values. Be honest with yourself so that you can find ways to incorporate your values in healthy ways. What values must be acknowledged and present so that life is meaningful to you?

Identifying the most essential values allow you to mindfully incorporate them in your decision-making. Although most of these values may be nice to have, which ones are most important to you? This principle is reflected in Gary Chapman's book *The Five Love Languages* (another great assessment). Love languages are ways in which people communicate and receive love. The five love languages are: 1) words of affirmation, 2) physical touch, 3) quality time, 4) acts of service, and 5) gifts.[60] Now most people want to experience love in all five ways, but they are not weighted equally! Probably one or two of these love expressions resonate more strongly, and if missing, you would not feel loved. For example, I

---

60   Chapman, G. D. (2015). *The 5 love languages*. Northfield Pub.

am a "words of affirmation" and "physical touch" kind of guy. If you give me a thoughtful gift, I would be appreciative and happy, but it would not carry the impact of affirmative words and physical affection. I tell my wife that I am a cheap date because saying, "You did a great job!" or getting a hug fills up my love tank...and it only costs her a few seconds! Just as we want our lives filled with the right love language (the one that matters to us most), we also want our everyday living to reflect the values that matter to us.

Another fun way to figure out your values is through a game called the Values Auction.[61] I played this game with teens in our hospital program. The game works best in larger groups because it increases the scarcity and competition! The facilitator presents a list of values and gives every person an imaginary $1,000 to bid. We used the following values: 1) A Comfortable Life, 2) Equality, 3) An Exciting Life, 4) Family Security, 5) Freedom, 6) Happiness, 7) Inner Harmony, 8) Mature Love, 9) National Security, 10) Pleasure, 11) Salvation, 12) Self-Respect, 13) Sense of Accomplishment, 14) Social Recognition, 15) True Friendship, and 16) Wisdom. The facilitator presents each value for auction and people bid for the ones

---

61   Values Auction: https://williamsghhs.files.wordpress. com/2014/09/day-2-values-auction.pdf

they want. The kids made a mental note of the ones they really wanted before the auction commenced. People's values get tested when other people are bidding against them. They have to decide in that moment, "How badly do I care about this value?" There were kids who bid their entire $1,000 on a single value like family. This reveals their clarity on what matters most to them. Some kids were too scared to bid and kept waiting for a better value until all the values were taken. Then there were kids who obtained several values because they got their secondary choices while winning other values at a bargain when other kids ran out of money. Those who were "saving" their money often ended up with nothing, given that the money was useless after the game was over. The game simply add a social dynamic and pressure that may help you identify the values that are most important.

Let me share with you my personal values. Through my own identity work, my decision-making is grounded on these principles. My beliefs about faith provide the foundation for my values. You do not need to ascribe to my perspective; I am not saying my viewpoint is the right way and it is certainly not absolute. It is where I have arrived thus far. Part of your journey is to discover who you are and your personal values. My intention in sharing my values is to provide an example of a life philosophy in hopes of inspiring you to discover your own.

I believe the purpose of life is found in God and my relationship with Him. As the creator of the universe and everything in it, God also created me for a purpose to fulfill in my short time on earth. Only He knows my true identity, strengths, and weaknesses. To know Him more is to know myself more accurately. My values are centered on God's values and perspective on life as revealed in the Bible. God does not need me to do anything, but He gives me the opportunity to partner with Him to love both myself and other people well. People are inherently valuable because God says so, which is why I see everyone as worthy of love and value. Love is my highest value. Love is a verb, an action to communicate and demonstrate care to humanity and entities around me. Since God is my heavenly father and king, then I am called to be His son and a prince, which comes with inherent dignity. My worth is not defined by what I do but rather who I am as His child. Some of those royal attributes include integrity, humility, and respect. He has given me talents and gifts in the area of communication and problem-solving. I can articulate complicated information into user-friendly ways for the purposes of equipping others to solve their own problems. My calling is to be a healer and restorer of individuals and their families. Being a psychologist is only a tool to do the sacred work of restoration. Why does that matter? Because God cares about making people whole. I believe in the Platinum Rule to "Treat others the way they want to be treated." That means taking the time to truly listen, understand people's needs, care for them on an emotional level, and communicate value and hope. I rank my highest priorities as tasks that only I can do and set healthy boundaries to protect them. I value relationships, first with God that then flows into loving my wife, family, friends, colleagues, and people. Issues arise when my conduct does not honor God, myself, or people. I reevaluate my actions to address inferior desires and recommit to my higher values.

You do not have to be religious or spiritual to formulate your values. There are great people in both history and the present who live honorably due to their professed and demonstrated values. People like Educator John Dewey (1859–1952) believed in the value of education and creating systems where people engaged their minds rather than mindlessly believing what they were told.[62] Or Marie Curie (1867–1934), a scientist who discovered radioactivity that led to the treatment of cancer.[63] There

---

62 Cherry, K. (2020). *John Dewey biography*. Very Well Mind. https://www.verywellmind.com/john-dewey-biography-1859-1952-2795515
63 Kułakowski A. (2011). The contribution of Marie Skłodowska-Curie to the development of modern oncology. *Analytical and Bioanalytical Chemistry*, 400(6), 1583–1586. https://doi.org/10.1007/s00216-011-4712-1

are people who have made huge contributions to society with different ideologies like Mahatma Gandhi, Anne Frank, Dalai Lama, Malala Yousafzai, and Alexander Hamilton to name a few. Whatever values you hold, take ownership of your identity. Through your true values, incorporate them in your optimal decisions. I cannot tell you what to value. Identity formation is a process. There is no rushing the development. With a hunger and curiosity to know yourself, create space to be known. Take time to consider and identify your own values.

Finally, I want to acknowledge death as a process to life. There is something beautiful about death that puts your life into proper perspective. Irvin Yalom, a psychiatrist known for existential psychology, said, "Death and life are interdependent: though the physicality of death destroys us, the idea of death saves us. Recognition of death contributes a sense of poignancy to life, provides a radical shift of life perspective, and can transport one from a mode of living characterized by diversions, tranquilization, and petty anxieties to a more authentic mode."[64] This is such a powerful idea. Though most people are terrified of death, the greater apprehension is to have never truly lived! Knowing our time on earth is limited spurs urgency to live your best life now. Do not wait

---

64   Yalom, I. D., & Yalom, B. (1998). *The Yalom reader*. Basic Books.

to take necessary risks, pursue personal growth, and love people well. Tomorrow is not guaranteed.

Live your life the way you want to be remembered. I personally believe people care about their legacy because there is something eternal placed inside each one of us. Ecclesiastes 3:11 captured this essence by stating God has "set eternity in the human heart." We were created with forever in mind and therefore, we care about our life's impact.

Lorraine Nilon said, "There is not a one-size-fits-all approach to living life, resolving the emotional baggage you carry, or accepting the truth of being an eternal soul."[65] You must form and discover your own path.

The last activity to consider is the obituary or eulogy exercise.[66] Imagine a room full of all the people you ever encountered in your lifetime. This would include the people you loved, folks who loved you, individuals who disliked you, strangers who briefly exchanged a hello, and everyone in between. Imagine these people attending your funeral as you sit in the front row. As various people come forward and share the impact you had on

---

65 Nilon, L. D., Hjorring, A. N., & Close, K. (2013). *Your insight and awareness book*. Insight and Awareness Pty.

66 Valentine, M. (2017). *How writing your own eulogy can help you follow your heart and live your best life*. Goalcast. https://www.goalcast.com/2017/10/09/how-writing-your-own-eulogy-can-help-you-live-your-best-life/

them, what would you want to hear? How will you be remembered? What did you do in your lifetime that mattered? Take some time to write down the desired statements people would say about your life. These are your ideal eulogies of a life well lived.

Then flip the script. I want you to imagine the most dreadful story someone shares about your life. This would be your anti-eulogy. What moment or incident would you hate to be remembered for? How have you hurt others? What actions would fill you up with guilt and shame? What would an unremarkable and fruitless life sound like? Take some time to write down what you would dread to hear. These are your nightmare eulogies of a disastrous life. Let those sobering thoughts sink in. Now take an inventory of your past week's thoughts and behaviors. Write down the thoughts you dwelled on the most, as well as specific actions that you took. Compare your past week's activities with the ideal eulogies. Do your actions align with your values? Will they contribute to the legacy you want to leave behind? Now compare your weekly inventory with the nightmare eulogies. Can you see how certain actions will influence the legacy you do not want? What are you doing that is working? What is the one thing that you are doing now that will not even matter a year from now? What priorities need to shift in order to create your desired legacy?

CONCLUSION

Whatever method you decide to execute, clarity on your identity and Values of Self is crucial for optimal decision-making. If you truly want to make optimal decisions, do not skip these exercises! There are no shortcuts. Identity formation requires dedication and hard work. Even if you managed only to identify one or two values, run with them for now! Keep those values in the forefront of your mind and incorporate them in your decisions. Values that truly matter will rise to the surface while inferior matters will drift into the background. Take the time to identify your values because your purpose depends on them. Your values become the north star in guiding your everyday decisions, which creates authenticity and greater self-esteem.

With a sharper understanding of your own values, the next factor is to navigate the reality that other people's values may or may not match your values.

CHAPTER 7

Values of Others: What Matters to Those Involved?

The majority of our conflicts occur because of ineffective communication. Shaunti Feldhahn, author of *The Surprising Secrets of Highly Happy Marriages*, shared an alarming statistic: "Even in struggling relationships, 97% of spouses said they cared about their mates. But more than four in ten believe their spouses don't care about them."[67] Why the discrepancy? Those spouses who believed their partners did not really care about

---

67   Feldhahn, S. (2013). *The surprising secrets of highly happy marriages: The little things that make a big difference.* Multnomah Books.

them interpreted missed expectations as being malicious. Moreover, their partner's "loving" behaviors were not being received as loving. There was a huge mismatch between good intentions and delivery. Our perceptions of what people want are not always accurate. Assumptions remind me that to "Assume makes an ASS out of U and ME." This is also true about the Values of Others.

We should not assume that people value the same things as us. There are general and common principles, such as people's need for respect, love, and acceptance. What may be different, however, is the *way* in which people want to be respected, loved, and accepted. For example, my father really enjoys spicy Chinese food. I dislike spicy food. If my father insists on serving me spicy Chinese food because he wants to give me his "best," we can see why that I would not receive that as a loving gesture despite his intentions. This goes back to the Platinum Rule of "Treating others the way they want to be treated," which is superior to the Golden Rule of "Treating others the way you want to be treated."

Why do we make these inaccurate assumptions? Because people perceive the world through their own sets of schemas, constructs, or "scripts." According to psychologist Jean Piaget, schemas are essentially our worldview of how we believe the world works. It is formed from early childhood and shaped by our life experiences.

Over time, we assume that our schemas must be how other people see the world too. A common schema may be "the world and the people in it are inherently selfish and untrustworthy."[68] With that underlying belief, you would instinctively behave more cautiously and doubt people's motives. The unintended consequence is your distrusting behaviors will cause a "vibe" where people are less likely to trust you. That reinforces your schema that "This confirms that people are crooked!" This is known as a self-fulfilling prophecy. The irony is that we are the ones creating the undesirable outcome! Stephen Covey stated, "We see the world, not as it is, but as we are—or, as we are conditioned to see it. When we open our mouths to describe what we see, we in effect describe ourselves, our perceptions, our paradigms."

Psychologist Jeffrey Young detected certain schemas that foster unhealthy relational dynamics, such as abandonment/instability, mistrust/abuse, emotional deprivation, and defectiveness/shame. Schemas left unchecked can drive poor decisions.[69] The *Oxford Dictionary of Sports, Science & Medicine* highlights the region of the

---

68   McLeod, S. (2018). *Jean Piaget's theory and stages of cognitive development*. Simply Psychology. https://www.simplypsychology.org/piaget.html.

69   Young, J. E., Klosko, J. S., & Weishaar, M. E. (2003). *Schema therapy: A practitioner's guide*. The Guilford Press.

brain called the Reticular Activating System (RAS), which is designed to filter out "unimportant" information while highlighting the evidence that fits your schema.[70] You will essentially find what you are looking for regardless of whether or not the belief is true.

To shift out of our schemas, we need to answer the question: "What are the Values of Others?" What matters to other people? What are their needs and wants? Consider what other people care about when generating your optimal decision. Like the saying "It takes two to tango," we want to work and move together. A "My way or the highway" mindset tends to work against mutually respectful relationships. Yes, we want to advocate for our own needs and speak up. The problem is when people address situations with *only* their own needs in mind. Optimal decisions require valiant efforts to create "win-win" solutions so everyone involved gets their needs met as well.

Like the whole spicy Chinese food analogy, we do not want to assume that people want what we want. Even if you guess correctly, verifying your answer can clarify both persons' expectations. My wife probably knows me the best. We have spent countless hours together and

---

70   Kent, M. (2006). *The Oxford dictionary of sports science & medicine*. Oxford University Press.

shared many experiences. She has intimately learned a not-so-attractive trait about me: I am a picky eater. What can I say? I know what I like! Sometimes my wife will order food on our behalf. Despite her knowing my go-to Vietnamese phở order is number 17 large, she still asks me, "What would you like to eat?" And I appreciate it, because it gives me a chance to clarify what I want so that she is sure about my needs. It is clear communication.

What if, when she asked me what I wanted, I said, "I do not know. Pick something for me." If I do this, I risk her choosing an unfavorable entrée. Whose fault would that be? Clearly mine. Am I entitled to feel disappointed? Sure. I could be secretly hoping my wife would "know me by now" and pick the "right" dish. But the fact is she *asked* me, and I told her to choose whatever she liked. The failure in communication is mine. Moral of the story: do not be lazy, and speak up. Even with people you know really well, take the extra effort to communicate your needs. Good communication is always relevant in healthy relationships.

Before reactively defending your own "rights," listen to the other person's needs and perspective. It is easy to get tunnel vision on what you want in the exchange. It is important to understand what the other person values and wants as well. In a situation where you have not met up with the other person, it is okay to ask yourself, "If I were in his or her position, what would I want?" This is the basis of empathy. Can you understand the other individual's goals and why they are important?

Imagine a situation between a father and his teenage daughter. The father agreed to let his daughter watch an evening movie with her friends. Both of them knew that the movie started at 9:30 p.m. and the daughter agreed to call her dad when the movie was over. When the daughter called her dad to pick her up from the movies, he was enraged! The father was upset because he thought the movie was over at midnight, but in actuality, it ended closer to 1:00 a.m. When he tried to call her during the movies, she did not receive his call because she had silenced her phone. The daughter fired back by saying, "I did nothing wrong! I did not know the movie was going to end that late either! I did exactly what we agreed upon." This led to a heated argument and a terrible drive home.

So, what went wrong? We can resolve the issue from a Values of Others perspective. What are the father's values? We can speculate that the father got visibly upset because he was worried. He valued his daughter's safety. Given that his daughter did not respond and it was 1:00 a.m., his anxiety led him to imagine scenes from the movie *Taken*, where his daughter is kidnapped and possibly killed.[71] What about the daughter? The daughter felt

---

71   Morel, P. (Director). (2008). *Taken* [Film]. 20th Century Fox.

offended because she was falsely accused of doing something wrong. She valued being respected and wanted his trust in her. With both individuals' values in mind, they can address the issue at the source of the problem. Assuming they value their relationship, the father can apologize for overreacting and explain that he feared something bad happened to her. If the daughter takes the high road, she can apologize for worrying him though that was never her intention. From a place of reconciliation and clear communication, she can agree to let him know "I am okay" through a text (as well as look into the length of future movies).

In many cases, offenses that feel personal are often not personal. We may feel like people are intentionally making our lives difficult. Yes, there are people who are internally miserable and take their frustrations out on others. Even in those cases, it is not personal! No, we are not justifying poor behaviors. We just want to remember that people are trying to fulfill their own values and needs as well. At the core, we can even sympathize with their needs and hurts. It is not all about you. When we acknowledge that people have needs like you and me, then we are able to step back and see the situation more objectively; we can shift our focus onto the actual issue.

Validation helps us understand the Values of Others. Validation is understanding what a person feels and why he or she feels that way.[72] It is communicating to another person, "That makes total sense why you would feel that way! How else are you supposed to feel?"

Formula: Identify the person's feelings + the why behind the feelings × reflect accurately = validation

For example, my coworker seems visibly upset. He is complaining about the payroll messing up his wage for the second time. Using the validation formula, break down the steps.

- **Identify the feeling:** My sense is that my coworker is frustrated and angry based on his raised voice and furrowed expression.
- **Why:** Because he did not get paid correctly for the second time. Take a moment to reflect. Does that make sense? Yes, I would be upset if I did not get paid for my work and the same mistake occurred again!
- **Communicate:** "You seem really pissed off that HR messed up your pay for the second time!

72   Vaughn, S. (n.d.). *DBT: Six levels of validation. Psychotherapy Academy.* https://psychotherapyacademy.org/dbt/six-levels-of-validation/

That sucks." In the situation where you reflect and cannot understand their feelings, ask questions to clarify. "It seems like you are really upset. What's up?" This exercise helps us build empathy and gets us closer to understanding their point of view.

Identifying the Values of Others can work with animals as well! Being able to identify that a dog is whimpering because he is scared allows me to put my energy into identifying the source of the fear and addressing the issue. The whimpering may be signaling fear. The value of the dog is security and safety. The dog needs the elimination of the feared object and/or comfort. If my focus is only on stopping the whimpering, I may yell, "Shut up!" and ignore the dog. By not addressing the root issue, the situation may worsen by causing the dog to whimper louder! And it is also mistreating the poor dog...not cool. Identifying the actual need and addressing the problem applies to any relationship: animals, plants, objects, and people alike! Can you see how identifying the Values of Others translates into how we treat others? Choosing validation helps our mindset address the needs or wants of others.

Acquiring the Values of Others may mean getting direct feedback from the people involved. If in doubt, check! There are many times when the answers you are seeking are literally right in front of you. "I wonder if she will like these pants." Want to be sure? Just ask her! If she is anything like my wife, she has a particular style and it is not worth the surprise if you are wrong. It seems an obvious and simple step to take, but it also may feel difficult to ask. If so, it is time to self-reflect. Why am I hesitant to ask? What is the fear trying to tell me? Maybe we do not want to kill the surprise. It lacks romance. Or asking the "common sense" question makes you look dumb. Maybe it is laziness. Not bothering to ask is simply easier. Want to make a decision based on a guess? Be my guest. Personally, I would rather be correct and let my efforts count.

I once had a candid conversation about communication with my then girlfriend (now wife). She seemed frustrated with me but I did not know why. She conveyed "the look" that indicated I had messed up. When I asked, "Is anything wrong?" she would not give me an answer. She expected me to figure it out! Apparently, the expectation was "obvious." So, I gave her a proposition. I told her, "I am training to be a psychologist, not a psychic. I can't read your mind! I don't know what you want unless you tell me. If you want me to be romantic by guessing your expectations, my hit-rate is probably two out of 10 times. I'll have a couple glorious moments but disappoint you the majority of the time. Or you can verbalize what you want and I will hit them 10 out of 10 times!" I know, not the most romantic conversation, but it fundamentally changed our relationship. Now, communication is one of our strongest qualities, and my wife is happy because I actually do what she wants. Although I have given her permission to be "bossy" (in her sweet kind of way), I am way less confused. If I do not agree with her opinion, we can actually have a discussion about it. She is also less resentful and disappointed. Over time, I have learned to pick up her patterns and take initiative regarding requests without her asking. A time may come when you no longer need to ask in a relationship because you just know...but, typically, that is not in the beginning! My commitment to prioritizing her values began with an invitation to know.

Our hope is that the people involved in your life know their own values. Sometimes they do. Other times, they are unable to articulate them. You may even suggest having them take their own value assessments! The ones mentioned earlier in the chapter can get any individual on the same page and speaking the same language. These people may include colleagues, teammates, spouses, and even kids. For instance, if your romantic partner also takes the Enneagram, both of you can develop a deeper understanding and appreciation of each other's unique qualities. Both persons can comprehend each other's mindsets based on their Enneagram profiles. There is now a common language to discuss one another's values in a more objective way! This is especially true with the Prepare/Enrich assessment, which compares both you and your romantic partner's values by putting them on the same scale to see similarities and differences.

There are times when you are unsure about the Values of Others and you are unable to ask the person directly. In these situations, the next best thing is to get feedback from trusted others who are not directly involved. The key word here is "trusted." Unfortunately, not everyone is trustworthy. Everyone is deserving of love and respect, but trust is earned. People genuinely want to believe they can be trusted with openness until their competing agenda causes them to betray you. When information is shared with untrustworthy people, gossip and manipulative behaviors occur to achieve some selfish gain at your expense. The resulting betrayal and abuse often leaves people hurt and less likely to trust at all.

It is crucial, therefore, to acquire feedback from the right people. Trustworthy people are those who have your best interests in mind—people who will give you accurate information to benefit you. Discussing situations with these trusted others can give you clarity. For a work situation, for example, discuss the possible wants and values with a trusted colleague. You are looking for specific feedback to get a pulse on the values of the people involved. The question may sound like, "What do you think the other person wants from the situation?" or "What does that individual care about?" This is different from asking, "What should I do?" You are not asking for their opinion of what you should do. You are gathering crucial information to make the optimal decision yourself. Compare and contrast the feedback with your initial thoughts about the Values of Others. This process allows you to get a more holistic perspective on the situation from a third-party observer.

Remember, conflicts are often differing priorities in values, not a personal attack. There is a difference in opinion about how something should be done. In many cases, both parties want the same things but differ on how to achieve the goal. For example, my wife and I are on vacation. We both have the value of having fun. The difference lies in "How do you define fun?" For my wife, fun looks like a packed trip with a wide variety of activities and restaurants for the "full experience." When I see the number of things to do and places to go, the vacation suddenly feels like stress and work! Although we both want to have fun, my version of fun contains less activities and at a slower pace. The conflict is that both paces cannot coexist while we travel together. She cannot do everything she wants and also do the relaxed vacation that I want. The difference in values is our definition of fun; my value for relaxation is higher than her value for excitement.

How do I honor her values while asserting mine? This requires a shift from scarcity to an abundant mindset. There are enough blessings for everyone! How can we honor both people? The answer often lies in the middle between your way and the other person's way. It is the undiscovered third option: the creative solution that works for everyone. These win-win solutions often exist in the shades of gray. It is neither black nor white, good or bad. It is no longer your way or my way, but our way. This third option is often a solution that develops when we review each other's values. No one likes compromises because it assumes everyone is settling and no one is happy. Not true! People can create win-win scenarios where both people are satisfied. The only prerequisite is an open mind to the possibility of being content with an answer that is not your initial idea. Even taking the time to create a third option demonstrates your Values of Others.

Back to our vacation issue. How can both my wife and I enjoy our desired vacation? How can we both value each other's fun? First, we look at my wife's list of desired activities to do in France. She has several museums, multiple restaurants, certain shops, different city neighborhoods, and nature sites. They all sound good to me, just not all of them in one trip! So, what are our options? One idea for a third option is to have her pick the top "must-do" activities with us together. For the other activities, I may stay at the hotel while she does those activities on her own or with friends. Or I may decide to check out certain shops of little interest to her and meet back together later. We have customized our pace so that my wife gets to do the majority of her list while I can slow my pace down. Without that collaborative problem-solving, we may both feel resentful about the vacation. Or we feel irritated at each other for "being inconsiderate" and argue throughout the trip. Why spend money and energy on a vacation that leaves our relationship worse? What a wasted trip to Paris, *oui*?

CONCLUSION

To sum up, people are inherently selfish creatures (including ourselves), so our optimal decisions must factor in how it benefits the people involved. Do not assume that "what is good for me is good for them." Get on the same page with each other. Our hesitation about the Values of Others comes from the fear that our own needs may be jeopardized. By shifting to an abundant mindset, we can discover a newfound option that honors both parties! Be open to creating win-win solutions that incorporate the other person's values as well. Based on the people involved and their responses, identify the values that are possibly present. Share what you imagine the other person values about the situation and fact-check your answer! The other person may even be shocked at your ability to identify their values before they do! Or you speculate incorrectly and ask for the correct information instead. When you stay curious about acquiring the Values of Others, most people cannot wait to tell you what they want. The aspirational goal is to work toward honoring everyone's values, which can only occur through communication and collaboration.

Now that we have identified our own feelings, our values, and the values of others, the final element of making optimal decisions is understanding the context in which these factors are contained. Our values and feelings intersect within a greater culture and society. Next, we will talk about the reality factors involved in our decision-making.

CHAPTER 8

Reality: What Are the Facts of What Is?

O nce upon a time, a thief wanted to steal a valuable bell in the center of town. One evening, when no one was around, he went to the bell. The bell was simply too large and heavy to steal in one piece, and so the thief swung his sledgehammer to break it. Instead, the bell rang loudly. Alarmed, the thief put on earplugs to dampen the noise and proceeded to hit the bell to smash it into smaller pieces. The more he hit, the more the bell rang, which led to the townspeople waking up and arresting him. You may be thinking, "What an idiot! Just because he cannot hear the bell ringing does not stop other people from hearing the noise!" This story is based on a Chinese idiom that roughly translates to "Covering Ears to Steal a Bell."[73] The moral of the story is that objective realities exist regardless of your acknowledgment. Ignore these realities and suffer the consequences. We may judge the foolish thief, and yet people ignore certain realities in their own lives, which leads to poor decisions and negative consequences.

Despite how unpleasant reality factors may be, we would be wise not to ignore them. People tend to reject or shut down reality factors that do not make sense to them. I often hear high schoolers complain about learning subjects that they "will never use in real life." The teen may say, "When will I ever need to know about algebra? I want to be a professional athlete! It doesn't make sense why I should care. I shouldn't have to learn it." Perhaps what they are really asking, on a more fundamental level, is "Why should I care about things that don't make sense? It just matters what I want or think, right?" Think again. It may be true that the student does not have to care about math. Despite his opinion on the matter, he still needs to pass the class in order to graduate. The last factor to

---

73   Li, H. (2018). 掩耳盗铃 *To cover one's ears whilst stealing a bell.* Ancient Chengyu. https://ancientchengyu.com/cover-ear-steal-bell/

consider is the reality we live in and its surrounding components. The reason why the information around us matters is because that is how the real world actually works. You can hate it. You can disagree with it. But it really does not matter how you feel about the facts. Facts are facts. As Bruce Hornsby & The Range sang in 1986: "That's just the way it is. Some things will never change."[74] The question is: do you want to work with reality in mind or fight tirelessly against it?

When I say reality factors, I am talking about how things currently stand. New information can shift reality, but you must work with what you know so far. There are factors like gravity. It does not matter if you do not believe in gravity. It does not matter if you do not fully understand gravity. If you decide to walk off a high cliff, you are probably going to die. Gravity will forcefully pull your body right smack down to the ground. These are the undeniable factors that make up our world, and wishful thinking is not going to change these realities.

When contemplating this step of the Framework, ask yourself, "What reality factors encompass the context of my situation?" There are different kinds of reality factors. The first category is observing your physical reality; this helps you gain objectivity. Physical reality factors are

---

74 Hornsby, B. A. (1986). The way it is [Song].

particularly important in decisions that involve physical interactions. Given that we have physical bodies and navigate through a physical world, it is important to take these factors into account. For example, factoring the weight and size of a couch (as well as your own physical condition) before deciding how to move it outside your room. Objective physical factors are gathered through your five senses: sight, sound, taste, smell, and touch. Keep your observations descriptive. Stick with adjectives such as colors, textures, weight, temperature, and size. You can begin with the location. Places can be anywhere from Disneyland to your own backyard. Describe the physical components within the place, such as trees, mountains, and the new skyscraper that is blocking your view. Identify the physical attributes of the objects in your world such as the density of the rock, the weight of the sofa you are moving into the living room, and the putrid smell from the two-week-old trash in the kitchen. Because this is not a discussion about philosophy, quantum physics, or psychosis, we are simply addressing the realities that exist within a healthy mind and person. A good way to check your physical reality is to see if your information matches with a trusted person's observations.

Although many of your tough challenges will not require physical factors to this level of specificity, the principle of objectivity will serve you well. Practicing the art of description will help you make better decisions. Oftentimes, our poor decisions come from assumptions that are wrong because we jumped to an "obvious" conclusion. For example, you may assume that the lady across the street is angry at you because of the expression she made while looking in your general direction. First of all, how do you know that the lady is angry? It may be her resting face. Or perhaps it is her thinking look. How do you know that she is angry at you? The lady may have a stomachache and is feeling sick. Maybe she is upset with the long line of people at the restaurant behind you. Imagine you felt offended because you perceived the lady was giving you a dirty look and cursed at her. To both your and her surprise, she looked shocked because she was never looking at you at all! That would be embarrassing. Remember, none of us are mind readers, so slow down and take a moment to describe the situation before making your assumption. Avoid judgments that categorize things into a good or bad bucket. This is especially toxic when we write off someone or something as being "bad" without taking the time to learn all the facts. There may be missed opportunities or misplaced judgments that occur when we fail to describe the situation first. Being descriptive allows you to put some distance between your thoughts and feelings. The lady in the previous example can be *described* as having her eyebrows pointed downward with a frown on her face.

That is it. Your task is to learn more. That description and pause creates an opportunity to evaluate the situation more clearly instead of making an incomplete conclusion.

The second category is the sociocultural reality. These factors consist of human constructs and measurements. This includes diversity factors, such as age, race, ethnicity, nationality, body size, disabilities, gender, socioeconomic status, education level, and family of origin. In our society, these influences have been given varying levels of value. Groups of people and the media communicate certain characteristics as desirable or not. Despite my belief that all people contain attributes of beauty and value, my neighbor may not see it the same way. We do not all need to agree on what attributes are good or bad. Just be mindful that society may have a differing perspective, which informs us on how we interact with people. We, too, have implicit and explicit beliefs about these realities that sway our thoughts and feelings. Remember schemas? Understanding our own prejudices and taking ownership of those thoughts can prevent unconscious decisions from being made (also known as implicit biases). When we increase our awareness around sociocultural influences, then we are able to take the first step in reevaluating those beliefs!

Another great way to identify reality factors is to list the influences within and outside of your control. This is also known as internal and external locus of control. Take a piece of paper and draw a line in the middle to form two columns. One column is titled "Factors within my control" and the other column is called "Factors outside of my control." For many people, the list of factors within your control is much shorter than the list of factors outside of your control. We cannot control the weather, our family members, our ethnicity, the opinions of others, or even how we feel in the moment. Welcome to reality. Most factors in our life are outside of our control! That list of factors outside of our control is the external reality in which we interact and incorporate our decision-making. The list of factors within our control is our internal reality, which we can directly influence. Some of those internal factors include the beliefs we choose to hold, our attitudes, and sometimes our breathing. The list of factors within our control may be limited, but it is the realm where our choices reside.

Do you need to identify all the reality factors before making a decision? Absolutely not. There are too many factors and not all of them apply to your decision-making (even for Sherlock Holmes). Part of mastering the Framework is knowing what information is crucial to consider and what is not relevant. If I am conflicted on what to bring to my neighbor's potluck, the fact that his door is red is irrelevant to my dilemma. On the other hand, everyone wearing black and formal clothing at a gathering except you may be important to note. There are certain factors that play crucial roles in making an optimal decision that should not be ignored. Unfortunately, prejudices and limitations exist. Awareness of these factors can help you decipher the most appropriate thing to say or do. I am not advocating decisions solely based on stereotypes or any particular emotion. Know what influences may be present and avoid any unnecessary ignorance. The goal is not to calculate everything, but to consider some possible responses and outcomes.

Cultural sensitivity is a practical way to incorporate reality factors. Unfortunately, I learned this the hard way. In 2017, I led a workshop on leadership development in Hungary. My team and I facilitated an exercise with over 60 participants who engaged in an imaginary society that evoked their unconscious values. The game involved money, power, and social status, which stirred up scarcity, stress, and competition among the people. After the game was complete, I shared my observations of the game and talked about the discrepancies in society today. The audience was primarily from First World nations, such as the United States, Canada, and Taiwan, so I addressed how their privileged status is connected with God's calling over their lives. After my talk, my cofacilitator sternly pulled me aside and shared that my message sounded offensive to the native Hungarians who came from poverty. The message unintentionally communicated that God's special calling was reserved for privileged individuals. I felt a drop in my gut as I recalled what was said. I was simply unaware of my entire audience and was culturally inappropriate to our host family. When we broke into smaller groups, I sheepishly walked over to the team from Hungary and apologized for what I had said. Thankfully, the team from Hungary was exceedingly gracious and understood the context of the talk. They did not interpret anything negatively or personally. After that experience, I have learned to increase my awareness about reality factors in any given situation.

CONCLUSION

Acknowledge that our reality can be altered by misperception. There are physical realities that are present regardless of our perception, but our interpretation of those realities is even more important. Dr. Phillip McGraw proposed that "There is no reality, only perception."[75] Even with facts, where we focus and how we interpret those factors shape our experiential reality. We accept that none of

---

75 McGraw, P. C. (2015). *Life strategies: Doing what works, doing what matters*. Hachette Books.

us are God and cannot know all things about any person or situation. There are strong limitations and we can only know a slice of a situation. Our own schemas and value systems can skew us into interpreting reality in a certain way. We want to avoid inferring a lady's frown as "She is mad at me," when in actuality, she has a migraine and happened to look your way. Start with your five senses and describe your observations before reading into the interpretation. Staying objective about reality factors can help you step back and think about other alternative interpretations. If in doubt, double-check your interpretations with a trusted other, such as a friend or counselor.

There are atypical circumstances that compel a decision that works against reality. On December 1, 1955, Rosa Parks refused to give up her seat on the bus because she was Black. She knew that the society around her was racist and the "separate but equal" laws unfairly gave priority to white people. Rosa acknowledged the reality of getting in trouble and the possible violence against her. After calculating the costs, she intentionally chose to stay in her seat. This led to her arrest and serial unemployment in Alabama.[76] Why did she do it? Rosa Parks con-

---

76   Stanford University: The Martin Luther King, Jr. Research and Education Institute. (n.d.). *Montgomery Bus Boycott*. https://kinginstitute.stanford.edu/encyclopedia/montgomery-bus-boycott

sidered the reality of culture and stuck with her value of justice, where giving up her seat because of her skin color was morally wrong. Her values superseded the cultural realities of racism. Her decision helped spark the nonviolent mass protests that drove the civil rights movement in America. Obviously, she did not want harm to befall her, yet repetitive discrimination was an intolerable reality. That is why reality factors are only a *part* of the equation. Rosa Parks considered the cost and made her true decision anyway. We need to make good decisions that are *informed* by reality factors, but those factors alone do not *dictate* our entire decisions.

We have now gone through four checkpoints of the Framework: Emotions, Values of Self, Values of Others, and Reality. Each chapter has unpacked what questions you need to ask yourself as you move through a checkpoint to better understand and evaluate the situation. With all these Framework questions at your disposal, it is time to put them together for optimal decision-making!

CHAPTER 9

Implementing the Framework

" I need an answer *now*! Cut the red wire or the blue wire. If you're wrong, the whole building explodes and all your loved ones die. You only have a few seconds to decide. Hurry up!"

Intense, huh? Those movie scenes get our adrenaline pumping because the protagonist is placed in a life-or-death situation. I remember watching a TV series titled *24* with this fictional character named Jack Bauer. As the director of the Counter Terrorist Unit, Bauer is responsible for protecting America within 24 hours.[77] Every minute counts

---

77 Surnow, J., & Cochran, R. (Writers). (2001, November 6). *24* [Television series]. Fox.

and decisions need to be made quickly. I have always wondered, "Does Jack never eat or use the restroom?" There are literally no pauses; just action one moment after another. Is that every moment of your life? Most likely not.

Our need to make a decision may feel urgent, but *rarely* do we have to decide right away. In fact, I believe the majority of our decisions can benefit from waiting. If we took a moment to pause and utilize the Framework, we would most likely make better decisions. I have met special agents and first responders who operate intense assignments and *most* of them have time to pause before leaping into action. Colin Powell's 40/70 rule suggests that humans need about 40% to 70% of the information for good decision-making. Gathering less than 40% of the information often leads to poor choices, but waiting for more than 70% may lead to missed opportunities. According to Dr. Steven Anderson, a leadership author and analyst, "The next time you have a tough decision to make, do what Colin Powell does, get enough information to make an informed decision and then trust your gut. You'll be glad you did."[78] The Framework gathers the essential information so your gut can make the right call.

---

78 Zaback, J. (2019). *Colin Powell's 40/70 approach to leadership and executive decisions.* LinkedIn. https://www.linkedin.com/pulse/colin-powells-4070-approach-leadership-executive-decisions-zaback/

In truly urgent situations, consider a modified Framework to make a quick decision. Sabrina Cohen-Hatton, Chief Fire Officer and author of *The Heat of the Moment*, developed a three-question protocol called "The Decision Control Process" for emergency responders to make a decision under pressure:

1. **Why am I doing this?** What is my ultimate goal in this situation, and will this decision help me reach it?

2. **What do I expect to happen?** How will this decision affect how the situation evolves?

3. **How do the benefits of this decision outweigh the risks?** Can you articulate these benefits in a clear way to yourself and those around you?[79]

These questions can assist in increasing situational awareness and decreasing human error. They can focus your attention on the problem and help you make a rapid call that breaks through fear and paralysis. Again, most

---

79 Cohen-Hatton, S. (2020). *The heat of the moment: A firefighter's stories of life and death decisions.* Black Swan.

of our decisions can be created more optimally through the Framework.

There are two dominant movements in the military: tactical and strategic. Tactical movement is used when "crap-hits-the-fan" and soldiers need to successfully navigate through the chaos. Rapid thinking and response are critical to prevent soldiers from losing their competitive edge, which could lead to death. The paradox is that even great tactical movement entails slow strategic planning and repetitive practice!

Back when I was in the Army Reserves, we had a squad of infantry soldiers demonstrate how to clear a room of insurgents during a training exercise. I was blown away at how high-speed those four soldiers moved! From lining up outside the door to occupying all four corners of the room with rifles raised took only a few seconds. It was incredibly fast! When my medical squad tried to clear the room, it was embarrassingly slow and awkward. Thank goodness our nation was not depending on our medical team for combat! The infantry soldiers were gracious to explain their speed: "We practiced countless hours of battle drills until we could do them in our sleep. So, when the bullets and chaos happen, we can automatically respond correctly with little thought." These soldiers demonstrated the power of making optimal decisions through the repetition and practice of healthy habits.

Strategic movement involves vision and planning. Picture a war room with several generals moving chess-like pieces across a map on a table. This is the aerial or bird's view. It is looking at the situation as a big picture and deciding what to do considering all of the components and keeping the goal in mind. Strategy cares about the purpose (the why) behind the actions and deductively decides what behaviors to implement to reach the desired outcome.

Optimal decision-making requires both strategy and tactics. The Framework is the strategy, and executing the decision is the tactical movement. If the tactical view is the trees, then strategy is the forest. As Chinese military strategist Sun Tzu observed in *The Art of War*: "Strategy without tactics is the slowest route to victory. Tactics without strategy is the noise before defeat."[80] One is not more important than the other, but strategy is like the preparation before engaging the war. The Framework helps us to see with intentions, values, and long-term goals before committing to any actionable decision. That is actually the role of our imagination! As human beings, we have the ability to think about potential scenarios and actions in our mind before acting on them. This is a huge benefit because no real consequences or

---

80   Sun-tzu, & Griffith, S. B. (1964). *The Art of War*. Clarendon Press.

resources have been expended when we think through our decisions before making them. We want to utilize our ability to use our mind to think through all the factors in the Framework, work through our options, and make an informed decision.

Although the Framework is not necessary for all decisions, most decisions can benefit from using it. For decisions that are based on preference, like deciding between chocolate or strawberry ice cream, dialing into feelings may be enough! You may not need to use all of the Framework. Working through the Framework may be quick when there are few factors to consider. Like in the ice cream flavor situation, other people's values are not involved because this is a personal decision (unless your partner wants you to share). The only factors to consider are how you feel about the flavors. What kind of qualities do you want (e.g., Do I want something sweeter? Or something creamier or fruitier?), and the reality factors (e.g., This place only takes cash; this shop only contains eight flavors, which limits my choices). The whole Framework process may only take you a minute to make your decision. Even so, consider practicing the Framework with minor decisions in preparation for the bigger decisions.

For the major decisions with serious consequences, using the Framework is a must. Pause. If you need a few minutes to think things over *before* making your decision, communicate your need for more time. Say, "Can you give me a moment?" or "Let me get back to you." People are often unaware of their perceived urgency and will demand an answer. Do not give in to their anxiety or impatience! For many of us, learning to set that boundary and using the Framework will be crucial to our optimal decision-making victory. One of the major advantages of using the Framework is that it forces you to slow down and check in with yourself before making any rash decisions.

Let us review. We are faced with a big decision and we are using the Framework to choose optimally. We start with our emotions: "How do I feel and why do I feel this way?" Your emotions (especially the more prominent and intense ones) are usually the primary indicator that the Framework is needed. Having strong feelings of anger, fear, or sadness tells you to pay attention to the situation and figure out why it is important.

After this, consider your own values: "What is most important to me?" Review your value system to see which values rise to the top in this particular situation. What bothers you is often linked to what matters. There are times when one value may supersede another value, but both of them cannot be expressed equally. For example, you may value speed in completing a task, as well as accuracy in doing a task. In a particular situation (like filing your taxes), the accuracy of the task is more important than the speed, despite your desire to finish the assignment quickly so you can do something else. Your Values of Self is determining how you want to show up and what you want to prioritize in any given situation.

Then advance to the Values of Others: "What is important to those involved?" If our aim is to create favorable win-win solutions, then we need to consider other people's needs, especially when their needs may not overlap with ours. In many cases, when we honor and fulfill the wishes of other people, the law of reciprocity rewards us with partnerships that meet our needs as well! This is particularly true when you honor the relationship above your personal agenda. Identify the other person's needs and wants in order to collaborate on ways to help them succeed. Take some time to learn about the person's goals by asking questions or researching the values of the organization.

Lastly, consider your context: "What reality factors do I need to consider?" We live in a real, physical world with resources and limitations. Wanting and wishing for things to happen is not enough! We have physical realities, as well as diversity factors that influence our culture and environment. Learn to work with what you have rather than what you do not have. Otherwise, we deceive ourselves and learn that what we want to manifest will not happen. If you are trying to accomplish something that has never been done before, bear in mind that certain reality factors are undetermined, so lead with your Values of Self as the primary indicator. Put all of the Framework information together in the simplest terms to give you a clearer overview of the problem. The optimal solution will often reveal itself as you sift through the Framework.

Using the Framework is a skill that is perfected over time. Like most skills, practice and revision is necessary for mastery. When anyone learns how to type for the first time, understanding the mechanics rarely translates into quick and accurate typing. Knowing the Framework is only half the equation. If this whole process feels clunky and weird, you are probably doing it right! Acquiring a new skill often feels unnatural in the beginning. You may need to review the questions. More time may be required to ask the deeper questions and understand your answers. You may have gathered inadequate information, so your decision is less than optimal. You may even arrive at the optimal solution but fail to choose it! All of these things are normal. Knowing is only half the battle! Implementation and follow-through is the other half. This is when courage and insight into your resistance are required to carry out the optimal decision. This will be covered in chapter 10. My encouragement is that, over time, using the Framework will become second nature. It is like a metaphorical muscle that you strengthen, and then you are able to think through the Framework with little-to-no effort! The Framework will become a part of how you process information on an unconscious level. As you fine-tune the process, your probability of making the optimal decision will continue to increase as well.

Now let us practice using the Framework. Imagine you are the leader of a design team for the latest Apple iPhone. There are multiple teams working together on this important project, and the deadline to roll out this product is in a few weeks. There is massive media coverage and great anticipation for the release of this cutting-edge phone. As your team is wrapping up their part in the project, you realize that there is an important piece of information missing from your report by the research department. This piece of information will determine how the iPhone will be built before being mass produced. Without that information, your team cannot proceed. Amir, the leader from the research department, is difficult to access as a colleague. You have already sent several emails and left a voicemail on his work phone but received no response. What should you do?

In this scenario, take a deep breath and review the Framework's information-gathering parts:

1. Emotions
2. Values of Self
3. Values of Others
4. Reality

Review each factor, identify what it is, and why it is that way. Emotions: Check in with yourself. How would you feel? Name the emotions. In this case, there may be a mixture of feelings. You may be feeling frustration and anxiety. Dig a little deeper. Why would you be feeling this way? The frustration signals unmet expectations, which feels unfair or wrong. What is your expectation? To lead your team into completing the project before the deadline with time to look things over. Instead, there is a holdup from the research team *and* the colleague with the answers is avoiding you. What is the anxiety signaling? Anxiety is a form of fear with restless energy to avoid a potential problem. What is the problem? That you may not meet the deadline, which will reflect poorly on both your team and yourself. It would also set the company back a few weeks because the product will not be ready to launch. Now your brain may have entertained the worst-case scenario where the failed product launch will discourage consumers, discredit the company brand, and get you fired. Your feelings are prompting a change to that negative trajectory.

Values of Self: What are my values? Since you have identified your general core values, review your list to see what matters the most in this situation. Values connected to the situation may include integrity, an ethic of hard work, peaceful relationships, excellence, and leadership. Define what each of these values mean to you. Integrity is being a person who means what they say and says what they mean. You aim to be a person who is congruent with your thoughts, feelings, and behaviors. An ethic of hard work reflects your willingness to do whatever is necessary to complete the project. Peaceful relationships involve working with colleagues in a kind and respectful manner. Excellence is doing the project at the highest level of quality and timeliness. Leadership is the value that tells you your team deserves attention and guidance to complete the project together. Examine your values and one can see how the anxiety and frustration reflects the concern of failing to live up to these values. Among these values, the most important one may be providing great leadership, which encompasses excellence, integrity, an ethic of hard work, and peaceful relationships.

Values of Others: What matters to the people involved? There are a few key players in this scenario. There are your teammates, who are working on the project with you, the lead from the other department, your boss, and other colleagues who make up the company. Think about the motivation fueling everyone's decisions. Your teammates probably value similar things as you, such as doing excellent work, meeting the deadline, and maybe gaining recognition for their hard work. Your boss and the people in the company probably value comparable values, such as having a successful and timely product launch, which will benefit the brand and the organization. What about Amir, the research department leader? If you were to speculate, what matters to this individual? Maybe Amir values accomplishment, which is why he is busy doing multiple things and is difficult to reach. Perhaps he has other priorities that need his attention besides this particular piece of the project. If in doubt, consider talking with a trusted colleague who knows him better. In this case, your colleague Thato knows that Amir is an "out of sight, out of mind" kind of person who is often late in responding to emails and calls. Thato believes Amir cares about excellent work and is highly ambitious for his next promotion.

Reality: What are the factors to consider in this situation? Some of the factors may include the work culture, personality factors, project factors, and limitations. The work culture seems fast moving, goal oriented, and team based. Amir's personality portrays a person who is an easygoing guy but takes weeks to return texts and emails. There are also other personalities within your team who have different strengths and weaknesses related to the project. You remember your colleague Stephanie has a good relationship with Amir and would be a better person to connect with him instead of you. The project has an approaching deadline, and it takes a few days to review before submitting it to the manufacturing department. The limitation to completing your project is the missing information from the research department. Another possible reality factor is that Amir and the research department believe that their report is complete and are unaware of any missing information.

With the gathered information, begin listing out your options. The core issue seems to boil down to getting the missing information for the project. As a leader, your responsibility is to obtain that information and set realistic expectations. There may be several ways to obtain that information. One option may be to assert yourself and request that information from Amir in person. Another option may be to go up the chain of command and contact Amir's boss and address the issue. Yet another option may be to have someone on your team like Stephanie ask another team member from the research department to get the missing information.

So, what is the right option? I do not know! Perhaps there is no right or wrong answer. In most cases, there is not a perfect answer. You did a great job of clarifying the issue and arriving at the possible options to solve the problem.

The purpose of the Framework is not about picking the fail-proof answer. It is about extrapolating vital information to help formulate creative solutions. If you were to ask me personally, I would probably select an option that integrates all those ideas. I would send an email to Amir about needing the research team's missing information while looping our boss in the email for accountability. To make matters clearer, I would get the original report and highlight the missing portion while also sharing how the report has been helpful in other ways. I would communicate with the team to create several mock designs in preparation for the missing information. I would ask Thato and Stephanie to reach out to the other research team members to either get the information or get ahold of Amir. Then I would set the next follow-up date while surrendering the aspects that are outside of my control.

Now the next few scenarios are based on real people and dilemmas. Read the scenario and practice using the Framework on your own before reading the character's response.

SCENARIO 1: "DON'T HOLD ME BACK!"

Sofia is a 30-year-old daughter from Mexico who currently lives at home with her mother and father. She has a strong desire to start her own business but her parents want her to take over the family restaurant, which has been passed down for four generations. Sofia has graduated from both university and graduate school overseas with the desire to use her education to start her business in Mexico. She cannot seem to stick to one business plan and has been jumping into different opportunities over the past several years with little success. Her close friend challenges her to take a risk and participate in a humanitarian trip to Africa to serve children for 10 days. She wants to participate in the trip, but it would use up the majority of her savings. Plus, this trip seems to have nothing to do with her career. Sofia's main concerns are:

1. Should I drop my current business endeavors to participate in this trip?
2. How do I get permission and support from my parents?
3. If I attend the trip, how do I attend without being financially ruined?

Pause. Practice using the Framework to formulate your answers.

Sofia's Framework

Emotions: I am feeling frustrated with both myself and my work situation because none of my plans have worked out so far. I am feeling confused because my business plans are unclear. I cannot decide on a plan because of my fear of failure. I do not want to disappoint my parents if my business never works out, and my pride will be shattered if I end up returning to the restaurant despite my education. I am also worried about attending the humanitarian trip to Africa with my close friend because the trip is expensive, and I may not have enough money to continue with my business ventures.

Values of Self: I value my independence and my ability to create something that has my unique personality embedded in my work. I want to prove to myself and other people that I have what it takes to be successful. I love my parents and the people who support me. I desire more clarity about my business and want to get out of this rut. I value boldness and courage to take hold of the good things in life. I trust God is watching over me and guiding my life.

Values of Others: My mother and father value family and traditions. They want me to be financially secure, healthy, and happy. My parents believe that taking over the family restaurant would provide that security just like it has for many of my family members. God values my trust in Him that He will take care of my needs and plans. My close friend wants me to participate in this trip to Africa because it would place me in a position of faith and a fresh perspective. She also values our relationship and wants me to share a unique experience in Africa with her.

Reality: The trip to Africa costs $2,000. My bank account has roughly $2,000. There is no guarantee that I will gain any more clarity about my business. I have a business idea right now, but I am still unsure about the idea. Venturing outside of my comfort zone is definitely an act of faith in God. My parents will most likely be disappointed if I do not listen to their desire to stay with the family business. A part of me will die if I stay in the family business and discontinue my own business pursuits. My parents love me regardless of my career choice. The opportunity to participate in this Africa trip occurs about once every three years.

Based on Sofia's Framework, she has a few options:

1. Give up on her dream by fulfilling her parents' wishes and work in the family business.
2. Continue working on her business plans and invest in more training and education.
3. Participate in the trip to Africa for a fresh perspective and live out her faith.

As you look at her options, there are benefits and costs to each of these decisions. Option one is maintaining the status quo to appease everyone but herself. Option two seems to be a reasonable choice, although she has not been successful in doing so the past few years due to a lack of direction. Option three seems to be the most aligned with her values given the Framework information. It involves exercising her faith and getting some distance from her current situation to gain a fresh perspective. Her decision is aligned with doing meaningful work, which may also bless those people in Africa and her close friend. Choosing to attend the trip to Africa may use up her finances and upset her parents. Given that Sofia loves her family, she may need to communicate her decision with her parents despite their opinion because she respects them. Option two may be the follow-up choice after returning from her trip. The final question: "Is this informed decision the best one I can make given the situation?"

SCENARIO 2: TAKE ONE FOR THE TEAM

Ramil is a 45-year-old husband to his wife, Rowena, and the father of three young children (Tala, Mayumi, and Crisanto). Ramil grew up with the mindset that the father is the primary bread winner, but his family has been struggling financially. He is currently doing random manual labor gigs in the city to make ends meet, but he enjoys the flexibility of spending time with his family.

Recently, Philippine National Oil Company offered him a job as an extraction crew member. The site is about a three-hour drive outside of the city. The job would be secure, and the pay would double his highest earnings. The work involves handling natural gas mining, which is pretty dangerous. The road conditions to work are terrible, which would encourage him to stay onsite during the weekdays and return home on the weekends. His burning question is simply "Do I take the job?"

Pause. Practice using the Framework to formulate your answers.

Ramil's Framework

Emotions: I feel pretty excited about the job offer that makes me twice as much money! I do not mind the change of scenery and the security of a full-time job. I notice some internal pressure to take the job as it would afford my family a better life. There is some sadness about the long work hours and missing time with my wife and kids. I also feel some anxiety about the dangerous work conditions, the treacherous commute, and being away from home on the weekdays.

Values of Self: I value responsibility and being a provider for my family. I am willing to put in the long hours and hard work if it means my family gets a better life. My family is really important to me, which means being able to spend time with them. I love the freedom to take my kids to school and laugh with my wife about silly things that occur during the day.

Values of Others: My wife wants me to provide for the family, but she has mixed feelings about me working in the oil fields because of the risks. She values my health and safety more than making more money because "money can be made in other ways." Rowena also shared her value of having a father present with the children. To her, it is important that I spend time with them. All of my children agreed that being away during the weekdays would make them really sad.

Reality: The constant "hustling" side gigs in the city is pretty stressful. The extraction crew job is pretty dangerous, which means I could get seriously hurt and even killed on the job. The new job would take a lot of time away from my family. The double pay would allow our family to pay off some debt and provide for my children's education so they could be better equipped for their future.

Based on Ramil's Framework, he came up with a few options:

1. Reject the offer and continue with his side gigs in the city.
2. Take the offer to make more money but sacrifice his safety and time with his family.

3. Reject the offer and become more proactive in seeking other job opportunities.
4. Take the offer for a season of time to pay off the debts and explore other job opportunities later.

As you may have noticed, Ramil's options are not that binary. His ultimate question is whether or not to take the job, but there is variability in the timeframe as well as other possible options for work. What Ramil needs to weigh out is if the financial security of his family is more important than his ability to spend time with his family. Again, there is no right or wrong answer as long as his options are grounded in his core values. Given that his family is important to him, this decision should probably be made as a family. The final question is: "Is this informed decision the best one I can make given the situation?"

SCENARIO 3: BUSINESS POWER MOVE

Gage is a 30-year-old business entrepreneur who oversees 13 employees. He grew up with both his father and grandfather being successful businessmen. Gage started his first business at the age of 21 and cultivated a successful tattoo parlor. He proceeded to expand his business and created three more shops. Gage works at the tattoo parlor for three full days to help out, but the shop is primarily run by a great manager and employees. In return, he pays them very well. Recently, he signed a new lease on a building to expand his business but suddenly five of his core employees decided to quit and start their own tattoo shop. His business income got reduced by 40%, which makes it difficult for him to pay his mortgage, rent the new building, pay his other employees, and maintain his livelihood. His questions include:

1. Do I take a loan in the hopes that my business will pick back up and I will be able to fill the five vacant tattoo artists' positions?
2. Do I take revenge on the five employees who left me without notice and crush my competitors before their business even takes off?
3. Do I sublease the new building and have another business operate besides mine?

In Gage's case, his initial thoughts have already come in the form of options and they are framed as a matter of yes or no. I would recommend putting those initial solutions to the side and utilizing the Framework first to formulate the solutions.

Pause. Practice using the Framework to formulate your answers.

Gage's Framework

Emotions: I am really mad at the five employees who left my business to start a tattoo shop in direct competition with me. I feel betrayed and sad that they did not discuss things with me first because I thought we were like family. There are feelings of frustration that my business plans are already in the hole with debt. I would have waited on the lease for the building if my ex-employees had discussed their plans with me. In a strange way, I do feel a sense of pride that my ex-employees are doing their own business because they were trained well in my shop. There is some anxiety about my finances, since most of my money is locked up into the business, and I still have bills and employees to pay.

Values of Self: I value success in my business, which means taking informed and calculated risks to make a profit. I pride myself in taking care of my employees and building businesses that have my unique signature. I value healthy friendships and partnerships. I believe in doing things the right way with integrity. I care about my image and reputation as an ethical businessman. I enjoy diversity and creativity in my work. I value high-quality staff because I know it is the best long-term strategy and fosters more enjoyable work interactions.

Values of Others: The ex-employees probably care about doing their own business with their own unique signature, like me. They want to be successful and probably did not tell me because of their aversion to conflict. Since I have been working with them for years, the ex-employees would ideally want to create a win-win scenario and leaving my business is most likely not a malicious attack against me. My current employees have their own needs and want to continue being paid. They continue working with me because they value our work culture that empowers them to do their best.

Reality: The new lease on the building is signed for a year and the first payment is in three weeks. I have enough money to pay for three months of the building. With the five employees leaving, there is a 40% reduction in cash flow, which will negatively affect my ability to pay the other eight employees. There may be a bailout or co-tenancy clause that would allow me to get out of the new building lease given the change in circumstances. It typically takes one to three months to vet and hire a high-quality and reputable tattoo artist, but it may take even longer. Clients come to my tattoo shops because of my unique branding and customer service. I have numerous testimonials and high online ratings for my shops, which will give me the competitive edge. The tattoo artists' world is a pretty tight circle and getting revenge on my ex-employees will only make our family culture unpleasant for everyone.

Based on Gage's Framework, here are a few options:

1. I can punish the employees who left me by using my connections to crush their business before it can take off.
2. I can value those relationships by sharing how they hurt me in hopes of supporting them and maintaining the family culture.
3. I can take a risk and hope to hire new tattoo artists in time so that my finances can fund the new building and expenses. If that does not work, then I could take a loan while continuing with those efforts.
4. I can swallow my pride and look toward subleasing a part or the whole building, put my own business ventures on hold, and get that money to support my current business.
5. I can find a way to get out of the new building altogether even if it means having to pay a penalty.

As you may see with Gage's options, two of the options address the relationships with the ex-employees, while the other three options address the financial issues regarding the building. Given the love for his tattoo community and his own value for entrepreneurship, he may want to reconnect with those ex-employees and make something work while being honest about his feelings. If Gage believes in his ability to hire good-quality tattoo artists, he may decide to plow forward and take the financial risks. He may choose to do so for a month before deciding to sublease the building. His solution may be to consider all of his options but execute them within different time intervals. Gage may decide to proactively hire new tattoo artists while looking for compatible new businesses to sublease the new building. Depending on the candidates who turn up in the next month, he can use that new information to decide whether to hire the new artists or sublease the building. Gage may decide to simply get out of the new building for now, take his time to hire high-quality tattoo artists, and then expand his business at a later time. Either way, he will be able to protect his current businesses and employees without gambling on potential new hires or businesses to sublease the building.

CONCLUSION

As I mentioned before, the Framework may not generate the perfect solution, but it will help you make an informed decision. It will allow you to consider the major factors that need to be addressed in order to make a good decision. At a minimum, the Framework will engender a dialogue with yourself and trusted others so that through the process, an optimal blend of options may present itself. The Framework also aims to filter out unnecessary noise and unhelpful rumination. The best answers often exist in the shades of gray, not the extreme black-and-whites, because we live in a complex world with complicated people. Hopefully, these few scenarios have demonstrated the Framework in action and what it may sound like in your mind.

Even if the best solution has been discovered through the Framework, it does not necessarily mean you will carry it out. There are psychological factors and circumstances that may hold us back from following through with our choices. In the next few chapters, we will discuss the importance of courage, recommitment, and ownership to achieve optimal decisions.

CHAPTER 10

Courage: Working Through Your Fears

have met many well-intentioned people in my life-time who know what to do and yet are unable to do it. Do you know people like that? They say all the right things and even give great advice, and yet continue living difficult lives. Saint Bernard of Clairvaux and other great thinkers believed that "The road to hell is paved with good intentions."[81] Wanting to do well and doing well are

---

81 QuotesCosmos (n.d.). The road to hell is paved with good
    intentions. https://medium.com/@QuotesCosmos/the-road-to-
    hell-is-paved-with-good-intentions-17326943c05a

two different things. There is a reason for this phenomenon. The common psychology adage states, "Insight does not equal change." *Knowing* better does not always translate into *doing* better. Brian Klemmer wrote a book on it: *If How To's Were Enough, We Would Be Skinny, Rich, and Happy.*[82] Tucker Max, a *New York Times* bestselling author, addressed the issue by saying, "The road to heaven is paved with good actions."[83] Knowledge is only powerful if you apply it. Take a moment to reflect on your own life. Do you always do what is good for you? If the answer is no, welcome to the humanity club. People are weird like that, are they not? I want to address this issue because using the Framework and arriving at the optimal solution does not automatically mean you will follow through with that decision. The more you are aware of this reality, the more empowered you will be to turn this situation around.

There are unseen forces at play when you are making a decision. Although Sigmund Freud had some pretty strange theories about the human psyche, he was able to describe our human experience in a way that resonated with people and helped them articulate their internal

82   Klemmer, B. (2005). *If how-to's were enough we would all be skinny, rich, & happy.* Insight.

83   Tuck, Edie. (2019). *You can keep your good intentions: It's the action that really matters.* Medium. https://medium.com/1-one-infinity/you-can-keep-your-good-intentions-80f32bf8744

conflict. Freud categorized the mind into three depart-
ments: id, ego, and superego.[84] Although these are not
literal parts of the brain, the theory strangely does a good
job of depicting the inner tensions in our mind.

The id is the raw, unfiltered entity that is filled with
intense emotions and desires. Imagine the id as a hyper-
sensitive 3-year-old child. The id wants to do what feels
right in the moment. You want that piece of cake? Yes,
and I want it *now*! You feel like slapping that authority
figure in the face? Then do it. That is the id. It is a bun-
dle of unconscious energy that is driven by primal needs
and instant gratification. The id senses urgency for all
its demands and does not care about the consequences,
until after the fact. You can probably see the downsides
of being driven by the id. Although those id-driven decisions may "feel" right in the moment, there are often
painful and unintended consequences. Guess who has
to clean up the mess? You. In Framework terms, these
decisions are only driven by the emotional department.

The superego is that moral, mature part of yourself that
aims to do what is right for yourself, other people, and society. You can picture the superego as a priest or saintly person.
It is your responsible, but often judgmental, older brother.

84   McLeod, S. (2019). *Id, ego, and superego.* Simply Psychology.
     https://www.simplypsychology.org/psyche.html

The decisions are based on fairness and health despite what you may feel. You may be thinking, "That should be our aspirational goal!" and, to some extent, you are right. The issue with a solely superego-driven mindset is that insincere decisions occur because the individual's desires are suppressed by what parents and/or society believe is right. The superego dismisses the id and aims to behave morally, even if the solution is unrealistic or false. This leads to living for the approval of other people while your own individuality gets silenced. In terms of the Framework, this is living a life primarily based on the Values of Others while ignoring the Emotions and Values of Self.

Lastly, the ego is the great mediator between the id and the superego whose aim is to negotiate both of their needs. You can think of the ego as the empathetic coach or the middle child who tries to keep the older and younger sibling from fighting. The ego wants to maintain peace by keeping the selfish little id and the overly righteous superego from killing each other. It considers the id's raw needs and the superego's "proper" needs by finding a socially appropriate way to satisfy both in its decision. The ego brokers both requests and tries to find a healthy medium that includes both parties. In Framework terms, the ego is primarily informed by Reality. The ego's blind spot, however, is its unhealthy assumption that stability and security are always good. This means that even if you are living a mediocre life, the ego does not want to "rock the boat" and jeopardize stability with any possible change. Change feels uncomfortable and is often interpreted as bad. Sometimes, the reality factors reveal limits and show what could be potentially good, but the ego would rather not push the limits and disrupt the status quo. When it is time to implement the Framework and follow through with positive change, the ego will often send strong signals to shut it down.

The ego has developed many creative ways to "maintain the peace" and avoid pain, even at the expense of your authentic self and problem resolution. I want to list common defense mechanisms that may come up when challenges arise.[85] Make a note of the ones that resonate with you.

- **Acceptance:** "I guess that's just the way it is" (even if there are ways to change the reality).

- **Acting out:** "&$@#* you! I don't care about you!" (This vents the emotion and diverts one's attention away from the deeper problem.)

---

85   85 Psychologist World. (n.d.). *31 Psychological Defense Mechanisms Explained.* https://www.psychologistworld.com/freud/defence-mechanisms-list

- **Altruism:** "Let me help you! Me? Don't worry about me." (This is a more pro-social way of avoiding the actual issues by focusing on taking care of other people's problems.)

- **Avoidance:** "I would rather not think about it right now." (This is the heart of procrastination, which delays the potential pain in exchange for short-term relief.)

- **Conversion:** "I just have this strange cough and tightening of my throat." (This psychological problem is expressed in a physically symbolic way. For example, the cough and tightening of the throat may represent the person's inability to speak up to her boss about unfair practices in the workplace.)

- **Denial:** "Problem? There is no problem!" (This is an example of creating an imaginary world where the problem does not exist or the responsibility for the problem is shifted away from the individual.)

- **Displacement:** "Why is my dog so annoying?" (This signals taking repressed feelings that cannot be expressed appropriately to the real person, like your boss, and taking them out on a safer entity.)

- **Fantasy:** "My life will be complete when she realizes her love for me." (This illustrates creating an overly simplified solution that is very unlikely to happen to solve a problem.)

- **Humor:** "I thought that shirt was weird anyways. Looks like something I wore in grade school!" (This is a more socially acceptable way to make light of something, but sometimes it dismisses how a person actually thinks and feels about the problem.).

- **Identification:** "Yeah, I wear Jordan basketball shoes just like the rest of my friends." (This adopts social norms or attitudes of people around you to avoid rejection or perceived threats.)

- **Intellectualization:** "Why should I feel sad? Dying is a natural part of life." (This focuses on the facts and normalizing a situation in order to detach yourself from uncomfortable emotions.)

- **Passive Aggressive:** "I guess only people who love me would have lent me the money." (By avoiding the fear of confrontation, it still communicates the person's feelings in an indirect way.)

- **Projection:** "I bet he hates working with children." (This shows how the person's unexpressed thoughts and feelings are placed onto another person, believing that other person must think or feel the same way too).

- **Rationalization:** "I only failed that test because the professor's questions were poorly stated." (By using excuses, you justify a person's decision or outcome instead of confronting the real reasons behind the outcome.)

- **Reaction Formation:** "I can't stand how everyone thinks that teacher is so pretty. She's ugly." (Although a person may have unacceptable thoughts and feelings toward someone or something, that person creates direct opposite thoughts and feelings to counteract his or her impulses.)

- **Repression:** "I feel uncomfortable about these romantic feelings toward a married woman."

(This is a common response to guilt and shame, where the mind pushes those thoughts out of awareness altogether, but they may show up in symbolic dreams or strange behaviors.)

- **Regression:** "Well, you're not my best friend anymore. I'll just eat ice cream by myself." (By reverting to more immature and childlike responses, the statement is associated with more secure and favorable times to alleviate stress.)

- **Social Comparison:** "At least I have a car that runs most of the time, unlike my friend who only has a bicycle." (This illustrates a way to feel better about someone's current situation by associating upward or negatively judging downward.)

- **Splitting:** "That cat of yours is nothing but trouble." (Simplifying things into good or bad, extreme black-and-white thinking makes it easier on the brain to think in more naïve terms.)

- **Somatization:** "I have really intense back pain after visiting my father." (In some cultures, physical or medical problems are more acceptable than mental and emotional problems, so the attention gets diverted to the bodily pain while unconsciously avoiding the real problem.)

- **Sublimation:** "I started a foundation to help families who lost a loved one to cancer in honor of my own daughter's battle with cancer." (By taking difficult experiences and channeling them in a positive way to address them, it is sometimes at the expense of really acknowledging the pain.)

- **Suppression:** "I refuse to walk by the liquor store because there is alcohol and cigarettes there." This statement reflects how a person consciously pushes away thoughts and feelings that are distressing. This is different from repression, which is unconsciously doing so.)

How many of these defense mechanisms are relatable to you? I have probably used most of these mechanisms at some point in time. The purpose of defense mechanisms is to help you navigate stressors and continue to function with minimal disruption. These responses are often unconscious, automatic, and abrupt. Our aim is not to avoid all defense mechanisms, but we also do not want to respond to life with only these mechanisms, because it takes power away from making intentional choices. If you look at it from another perspective, you will see that defense mechanisms often occur when a real issue needs to be addressed. Thus, similar to emotions, the more we are aware of these mechanisms and their role in obscuring the real problem, the more we are able to slow down and utilize the Framework to work through the main issue. Although confronting these issues may cause distress, we must make the unconscious more conscious so we can deal with our problems properly.

This is why Courage is the final checkpoint to the Framework. Once the Emotions, Values of Self, Values of Others, and Reality have been integrated to identify the optimal decision, courage is required for action. Often, anxiety and fear will arise and self-doubt will take over your brain because change feels unsafe. "What if my decision doesn't improve my situation?" "What if I make this decision and the problem gets worse?" "What if people exclude me for asserting myself?" "What if this isn't even the best choice?" Then the failure to execute a decision due to overthinking ruins all your hard work as you put the decision on the back burner.

Fear and hesitation are natural responses! Not every optimal decision will feel good. There are times when you experience the pressure lift from your shoulders once you make a decision; those are the slam dunk cases, where you feel energized and empowered! Other decisions, however, conflict with your ego and feel really scary. Why? Because decisions evoke movement and consequences. Notice the mental and emotion defense mechanisms that may be showing up to prevent you from taking action. Remember that the alternative is also true: there are consequences for your inaction as well. Remember that every decision or lack thereof will have repercussions. Staying the same can also perpetuate problems. Inaction will keep you stuck in a less-than-optimal situation without a fight. Do not live life wondering if things would have improved. Time, our most precious resource, will keep marching on and never come back. Life is short, and we do not know how much time is left. Identify the cause of the fear, the potential consequences, and the importance of this decision despite the potential consequences. Practice calling out the fear and declaring the truth that living authentically is more valuable than staying the same.

How do you amplify courage? There are several ways that can help you follow through with your optimal decision. We are no longer asking, "What should I do?" but "What is keeping me from doing it?" Courage is the fifth checkpoint of the Framework when there is decisional resistance. Walk through the Framework once more to uncover the core struggle. Examine your emotions. What emotion is present? Why do you feel resistant? Appraise the Values of Others and reality factors. What do I believe will happen if I speak up? Who will be most affected by my decision? Imagine your worst-case scenario. How terrible is it? Irrational? Highly probable? Make an evaluation of how realistic those consequences may be. Better yet, say those consequences out loud or write them down on a piece of paper. This will provide more objectivity and put some distance between your thoughts and your feelings.

Now imagine the aftermath if you choose not to make a decision. Imagine you loved an individual for many years but never had the courage to share how you felt. What would happen? The person would never know. That individual may end up with someone else, move away, or die without a clue. You would live with the regret of never knowing if an intimate relationship with that person was ever possible. Let that sink in for a moment. How does that feel? Are you really okay with that outcome? Reflecting on a reality where your goals are never achieved can help put your inaction into perspective.

Your resistance may be the result of a phenomenon known as the "sunk cost effect." People resist healthy changes to justify past losses. Imagine you bought a car for $100. It is too good of a deal to pass up! You get into your new car and drive it for a few minutes before your car breaks down. You go to a mechanic and learn that something broke inside the car. The mechanic tells you the repair will cost you $250. You have a dilemma. Do you fix the car? If you choose not to fix the car, then you would have to admit that you wasted $100. If you choose to fix the car, the total cost of the car is now $350, which is still cheap for an automobile, right? So, you decide to fix the car and you are back on the road. You drive the car a few more miles and it breaks down again. The mechanic tells you the repair will cost another $500. You are back to the same dilemma. These cars are called lemons. They are unreliable cars that will cost you more than they are worth. It is not just in money but also in time, energy, and pain. What keeps people trapped in "repairing" is the hope of redemption and the avoidance of being wrong. Are you in a lemon situation?

Whatever dilemma you face, fight the sunk-cost effect; do not let it prevent you from acting. Remember the past costs *and* the future costs of maintaining poor decisions. It is not worth perpetuating a bad situation further in order to recover lost time and resources. Inaction is similar to how Ravi Zacharias, author and Christian apologist, depicts sin: "Sin will take you farther than you want to go, keep you longer than you want to stay, and cost you more than you want to pay."[86] If sameness does not really

---

86 Terkeurst, L. (2018). *The slippery slope*. Crosswalk. https://www.crosswalk.com/devotionals/encouragement/encouragement-for-today-december-6-2018.html

bother you, perhaps the situation is not that important. Good feedback! But remember that your ego can also justify and convince you to keep things the same, so be brutally honest with yourself. Are you really okay with sameness? You can lie to people and they may or may not eventually find out. But when you lie to yourself, no one can save you. Do not fall prey to the lie that indecision is a crimeless act. Your future self is at stake. Use the guilt, pain, and regret as motivation to change. I define failure as giving up on yourself. As long as you are willing to make a call, you will never fail.

As encouragement, imagine your optimal decision working in your favor! You ask the person who you really like on a date and the person says yes. The project you have been working on for several years gets international recognition. You win the election against a popular opponent. Many families are saved because of your efforts to provide drinking water. Your conversation led a hopeless loved one to find an unwavering reason to live. How would that experience feel? These aspirational desires can be summed up in one word: vision. It is setting a clear intention of what you want to create.

Olympians do visualization exercises as part of their training. They meditate on the process of their event and envision their victory. The brain registers the success as valid and unconsciously finds ways to realize it.

Acknowledge that positive outcomes are equally possible! We give so much credence to our worst-case scenarios but spend little to no time on the best-case scenarios. Both positive and negative consequences are possible. What is the best outcome that may come from your authentic choice? How would you feel if things worked out? Does that reality excite you? Would you experience more peace of mind?

Now anchor your actions to your Values of Self. What truly matters to you in life? What kind of person do you aspire to be? Every decision, both great and small, will either add or take away from who you desire to be. Gandhi shared the impact of decisions in this way:

Your beliefs become your thoughts,
Your thoughts become your words,
Your words become your actions,
Your actions become your habits,
Your habits become your values,
Your values become your destiny.[87]

A meaningful life is a values-driven life. How do you live a rich and beautiful life? Live according to your values. Life is too precious for inauthentic decisions. Every time

---

87   Quotes.net. (n.d.). https://www.quotes.net/quote/41782

you choose an action that is aligned with your values, you are transforming into your best self. Do not despise humble beginnings, for all great people are an accumulation of their healthy decisions, especially during adversity.

Talk yourself into courage. Saying your optimal decision out loud can be a catalyst for action. Sometimes well-intended people voice their fears through discouragement and opposition. Recenter your voice. Emphasize your core values and use them as a weapon against doubts. We must remind ourselves of what is most important to our life. Develop a mantra, watchword, or short phrase that you repeat when resistance is overwhelming. Statements that are action-oriented usually work best! For example, imagine you got into a huge fight with your parents. After a few weeks, you no longer want the relationship to be strained. Every time you think about calling them, distressing emotions cause you to stop. A simple mantra may be, "No regrets. Call them now." Say it over and over again. "No regrets. Call now. No regrets. Call now."

When my wife and I were taking care of our newborn son, both of us were sleep-deprived and irritable. My seasonal watchword was "service." I would ask myself, "How can I be of service to my wife and son?" Whenever I said the word "service" to myself, it would shift my focus back to taking care of my family rather than getting wrapped up with my dissatisfaction. The mantra is an intervention to stop your brain from overthinking. That self-talk can short circuit the extraneous noise in your mind and anchor your thoughts back to your optimal decision. You can test a few mantras and see which one resonates with you the most. Remember, keep the mantra short or else it is difficult to repeat! And keep in mind that the Courage checkpoint is not the time to think about your options. Trust the work completed through the Framework.

Call out your past victories. Highlight a time when you were able to do something successfully. It can be something as simple as a daily follow-through like brushing your teeth or eating breakfast. For those who have experienced milestone accomplishments, meditate on those moments. They may include graduations, overcoming a hardship, receiving a reward, or doing something meaningful. Pause. Take a moment to revisit how you felt and what that accomplishment means to you. Your success history can help "pump you up" for action once more. Let your successes serve as a reminder that you have what it takes to become a person of integrity. If you could do it before, you most certainly can do it again! Often our fears settle in because we have forgotten who we are and how far we have come to be at this exact moment. Do not forget to balance your setbacks with past winnings. Courage is only a choice away.

If no past successes come to mind, change it now by making the right decision! The opportunity to shift your destiny is upon you, one decision at a time. You can change the trajectory of your future with your next choice. Perhaps your family lineage has a history of cheating or using drugs. You can break that generational curse by choosing differently. The next generation is counting on you. Every choice that gets you closer to your desired self is a win! You do not have to execute the Framework perfectly. When you are clear about your values and action plan, following through is what ultimately matters. Carl Jung, founder of analytical psychology, believed, "You are what you do, not what you say you'll do."[88]

Lastly, courage does not need to be achieved alone. Countless people in my life like my parents, mentors, and friends have encouraged me during my moments of hardship to continue fighting. Who are the people in your life who love and believe in you? When we cannot talk ourselves into courage, sometimes the encouragement of a loved one can spur us into doing the right thing. Many of our battles do not have to be fought alone. Although you are the person making the challenging decision, courage preparation does not have to be a solo thing. Call upon

88 Quotable Quote. (n.d.). https://www.goodreads.com/
    quotes/3240-you-are-what-you-do-not-what-you-say-you-ll

those trusted people to speak up in your life. You can review the Framework process with these individuals and discuss how you arrived at your conclusion. Allow people who have your best interests at heart to admonish you to live out your values through encouraging words, positive thoughts, and/or prayers. They may even provide a fresh perspective or additional information that can further clarify your resolve. Many times, our greatness is the result of the people who support us in becoming our best selves. Isaac Newton once said, "If I have seen further, it is by standing on the shoulders of giants." Draw courage from wherever you can find it and dare to move forward.

When the optimal decision and courage are finalized, then it is time to act. Thinking more will add little to no value. There is a point in time when thinking will prevent you from accomplishing your goals. Remember, if you have already utilized the Framework and identified the optimal decision, then being entrenched in analysis will become a barrier. Overthinking is an active excuse for inaction, a façade for delaying potential consequences. This often occurs when I am at the gym. My exercise activities are predetermined for that day. Before I begin or when I am in the middle of doing an exercise, I notice my brain starts telling me reasons to stop. I come up with a variety of reasons, such as "Being at the gym is what matters. You don't have to complete that set" or "What if you just skip that exercise? You did enough for today." I will admit, sometimes I listen. Other times, I choose to revisit my goals, push aside the unhelpful self-talk, and "just do it." Stick to the plan. Stop analyzing. Focus on the action. This is one of the few moments where "turning off your brain" is most advantageous to staying the course. This is not the decision-making phase; it is the doing phase. Do not give into the reevaluation trap. Instead, have faith that the Framework process has identified the best course of action. It is time to act and engage.

CONCLUSION

Courage is executing your optimal decisions despite the discomfort. Nelson Mandela, who was President of South Africa and an antiapartheid revolutionary, said, "Courage is not the absence of fear, but the triumph over it. The brave man is not he who does not feel afraid, but he who conquers that fear."[89] When insecurities paralyze you, remember your values and why your optimal decision is so important. Identify past successes to encourage your future behaviors. For some of you, dare to step into your greatness for the first time. Have trusted individuals

---

89 Quotable Quote. (n.d.). https://www.goodreads.com/quotes/5156-
i-learned-that-courage-was-not-the-absence-of-fear

speak affirming truths to infuse you with the needed courage to bring your optimal decision to completion. As John Mayer captures in his song "Say":

Have no fear for giving in
Have no fear for giving over
You'd better know that in the end
It's better to say too much
Than never say what you need to say again.[90]

Now, we also want to prepare for less-than-optimal outcomes. It is a huge accomplishment to work through the Framework, identify the best choice, and put that decision into action. Unfortunately, that does not guarantee success. What happens if your decision does not work out as planned? What do you do when your optimal choice was not a great choice? What if you make a poor decision despite your best efforts? In the next chapter, we will explore how to rebound.

90 Mayer, J. (2007). Say [Song]. On *Continuum* [Album]. Columbia Records.

CHAPTER 11

Rebound: What to Do When You Make a Bad Decision

I t is never too late. William was born in 1984 in a poor Roma village in Hungary. His single mother could not raise him and left him and his siblings with their grandparents. His grandparents were harsh and abusive toward him. By 14, he had dropped out of school and run away from home. William got involved in a life of crime. He started with petty theft, became a mule to push drugs, and worked his way up to becoming a mob boss and night club owner in his area. At the height of his power, he was the top drug and human trafficker in Eastern Europe among the Gypsy people. Despite being a feared man in his city, he found himself constantly angry, empty, and alone.

When he was 28 years old, his oldest son asked him, "Why are you sad all the time and drinking?" Something inside of him broke and he began sobbing. Eventually, he fell asleep and woke up to a man dressed in white next to his bed. Utterly shocked, he asked, "Who are you? What are you doing in my room?" The man told him to go down the street to a church and find out. It happened to be a Sunday morning and William learned that the man sitting next to his bed was Jesus. After that encounter, he completely turned his life around. William gave up his previous lifestyle of drugs, sex, and alcohol so he could learn more about his faith. He is now a passionate pastor of a church with over 100 members, sharing the good news, healing the sick, and raising the dead. How would I know? I had breakfast with William in Pécs, Hungary, back in 2017. Regardless of your views on William's encounter with God, his story showed me that lives can be turned around—for some people, in an instant! What really matters is starting with a single choice to do things right. Rocky Balboa said it best, "It ain't how hard you can hit. It's how hard you can get hit and keeping moving forward."[91]

---

91   Stallone, S. (Director). (2006). *Rocky Balboa* [Film]. United States: Metro-Goldwyn-Mayer Columbia Pictures Revolution Studios Chartoff/Winkler Productions. YouTube. Retrieved 2020 from https://www.youtube.com/watch?v=D_Vg4uyYwEk

Who is your hero? Maybe the person is a historical figure like Abraham Lincoln. Perhaps it is a fictional character like Wonder Woman or Gandalf from *Lord of the Rings*. Or maybe it is a rescue or service animal. A common trait of a hero is the confrontation of an overwhelming challenge and the power to overcome it. Imagine watching a movie where the hero has no problems or solves the challenge with ease. You would probably stop watching that movie early on because the story would be boring! In fact, a hero would not be a hero without overcoming a challenge that helped someone else. The individual might be a "nice" person, but most certainly not a hero.

Whether we are aware of it or not, we are the hero in our own stories. Christopher Reeve, the original actor for *Superman*, stated, "A hero is someone who, in spite of weakness, doubt, or not always knowing the answers, goes ahead and overcomes anyway."[92] It is the same in life. We experience various challenges throughout our journeys and do our best to overcome them. We are not perfect, but neither are our heroes. In fact, the heroes that resonate the most with us are those with blatant flaws—Batman, Han Solo, Sherlock Holmes. These are

92 Quotable Quote. (n.d.). https://www.goodreads.com/quotes/1514493-a-hero-is-someone-who-in-spite-of-weakness-doubt

main characters who do not act like typical heroes, are often misunderstood by the public, and yet they have good within them. They cannot use the traditional ways to solve problems because of their conundrum (like being a criminal, for instance), yet they get pulled into a story where their values direct them to do what is right.

Like the heroes in fictional stories, we will make mistakes. We will not get everything right the first time. In fact, failure is a huge part of the process! Often, by making mistakes, we learn what not to do and modify our approach the next time. Using the Framework guidelines will help you make better decisions, but it cannot guarantee mistake-free decision-making. No framework can do that. It is simply a tool to identify the major factors that are important in decision-making, increasing your odds on a desirable outcome. Unfortunately, there is one variable that can mess up even the most perfect plan. That is right, the human part. To err is to be human. Our choices will still contain flaws. Here are a few reasons why an "optimal" decision may still end up with poor outcomes.

1. **Missing crucial information**. We can only make the best decision with what we know at the time. Then we learn new information that totally changes the situation. I saw a client who sought treatment for her depression and anxiety. A year

into seeing her, she was not getting any better. Then the client revealed that she was sexually abused by her father who continues to live with her today. That piece of information considerably changed the approach of my counseling because I learned that trauma is at the root of her symptoms and she is being triggered every day. It happens. Crucial information can be hidden from us. Differing information may also reveal itself after we have made our decision. We just cannot know everything there is to know about a situation before making a decision. If you needed to know everything about something in order to make a decision, you would never make a decision. You need to have self-compassion and acknowledge that you did your best with what was available at the moment; you could not have prevented this undesirable outcome.

2. **Inaccurate information**. You may use the Framework and end up gathering inaccurate information. Even with good intentions, sometimes people give you the wrong information. You get misinformed and make a call that does not match reality. There are instances where people are purposely giving

you bad information to sabotage your success. My sister once told me that her college was particularly competitive but "everyone seemed so nice." In one particular science class, the grades were based on a curve so that the highest grade would be the new 100%. She met certain students who would "help" other students by giving them the wrong answers, hoping that it would lower the curve. That is why doing your due diligence by fact-checking is so important!

3. **Poor predictions.** Even with the best intentions, there are times when we simply speculated and guessed wrong. All of the data suggested the company would do well, but an international pandemic changed that reality. The opposite also occurs when a large percentage of stock analysts predict a certain company's failure. The company stocks continue to succeed regardless of the negative statistics. Or you assumed your teenager would appreciate items with cats on it because of her love for cats. When you gave her the "cool" cat backpack for her birthday, you learned that her love for real cats did not translate into cat things. This is a misinterpretation of information that led to an inaccurate conclusion. What we thought

was a calculated prediction still turned out to be wrong. The disappointing results occurred because your prediction did not match up to what actually happened.

4. **Lying to yourself.** Self-deception is the most difficult thing to figure out. You do not know what you do not know. When you have convinced yourself about something untrue, then no one can help you. The Framework will not be helpful if your Values of Self are simply not true. This is like establishing the wrong destination and somehow expecting to arrive at the right one. Our values-driven north star is our primary guide! Do not let other people or society define what is valuable to you. You may lie to yourself that something does or does not matter, but your emotions and even body sensations will start revealing discontentment. The negative outcome may be linked to unawareness around what truly matters to you. That unconscious mind block may be preventing your best efforts in doing the proper work. The only way to prevent self-deception is to be honest with yourself. For some people, recognizing your own voice may take more intentionality and time. Trust the process.

HANDLING GUILT AND SHAME

Guilt and shame are common responses after a poor decision. Guilt is a heavy feeling of regret when we do something wrong. It is about feeling uneasy for hurting or disappointing oneself or others. Feeling guilty is not necessarily a bad thing! It is informing you that unintended consequences have occurred, and you are being responsible for your part. Taking responsibility can be really difficult for people because there is a cost for making things right. That includes admitting fault, which bruises the ego. It also puts a person in a vulnerable state to be further criticized or rejected. Why do it? Because responsibility sets you up for the next optimal decision. Sociopaths and psychopaths, by definition, are unable to feel empathy or remorse. These people are only interested in satisfying their own goals regardless of who they hurt in the process. Their lack of guilt is the problem! Allow yourself to feel the guilt and use that energy to make things as right as possible.

In contrast, shame is damaging and unhelpful. Whereas guilt is feeling bad for doing something wrong, shame is feeling awful about being *someone* wrong. It is a disgust with oneself and the need to keep that bad part hidden. Shame is personalized guilt. It is usually the accumulation of negative feedback over a course of time that leads someone to conclude that "I am the problem." If people are trapped in feelings of shame with the core belief that they are the problem, then making optimal decisions becomes increasingly difficult. People who embody shame tend to unconsciously make poor decisions because it feels congruent. There is an unspoken expectation that bad people make bad decisions, even when the conscious mind truly wants to make good decisions. That is the subtle danger of shame. Someone who is consumed with shame will struggle to make good decisions; it is like trying to clean a table with a dirty rag.

I remember eating at this local Vietnamese restaurant and watching the worker "clean the table." The more the person used the dirty rag to sweep the table, the more filth was being spread on the surface. Remember, good people still make bad decisions. Do not let shame define you. It has no part in becoming your best self. We are all in need of more grace and do-overs. Choose not to allow past poor choices to define your identity.

Our guilt and shame often come from the good intention of self-improvement. We unconsciously think, "I will make myself feel so bad that I will never make that mistake again." It is also our innate sense of justice that someone needs to be blamed for the mistake and take responsibility. For many of us, self-criticism makes us feel terrible, but it does not always elicit change the next time the challenge occurs. People tend to have poor emotional memory, so when the temptation of bad choices shows up, our brain forgets *how* bad it felt the last time we made that mistake. In fact, we are more likely to remember the "benefits" of the bad choice and ignore the consequences. So, what is the point of punishing ourselves? Little to nothing. Our fear-based guilt and shame may be helpful temporarily, but detrimental for our long-term well-being. Our minds unconsciously begin putting the negative experiences together and conclude that we are the common denominator (which will always be true since you are involved in every one of your decisions). The shame begins creeping in and we inaccurately conclude that we must be screwed-up people. When the shame becomes a more permanent fixture, the belief that you will always mess up because you are messed up gets solidified. Hopelessness and apathy set in, and there is no more courage to try again. So how does that help you with making optimal decisions? It does not. Guilt and self-criticism often lead to giving up the Framework and reverting to lazy thinking and behaviors instead of allowing your decisions to flow from your identity and values.

Practice self-compassion and accept that imperfections will occur. This will be a tough one for control freaks and perfectionists! In order to break out of the negative loop, we must accept that mistakes happen *and* we can do better next time. In fact, why should mistakes not happen? Expect it. Acknowledge your humanity. People make mistakes...all the time. Take some time to understand the intentions behind your decision. The pain is often worse when we have good intentions and the outcome still comes out poorly. Other times, we do not always have the best intentions either. Acknowledge that reality too! For self-compassion, be gentle and kind to yourself. Check your internal dialogue. For a moment, put any self-criticism to the side and deal with it later. Notice any emotions that arise. Give yourself permission to feel those feelings. Speak to yourself with grace. In your particular situation, can you see why it makes sense that things turned out this way? Follow the sequence of events, and give yourself permission to explain the outcome. Take the observer stance to describe what happened. Put the situation into perspective and include all the factors that created the "perfect storm." List the reality factors. For example: "I missed my daughter's soccer game (again) because I miscalculated the traffic and chose to wrap up my project instead of leaving earlier." Frame the situation in an "I" statement because you are choosing to take ownership of your role in the situation. Yes, there are real life challenges like traffic and work. This is not making up excuses or shifting responsibility! We are simply acknowledging what happened. Reality factors do not take away your responsibility. When you own your role while taking reality factors into consideration, you can normalize the outcome. Taking ownership of your role keeps you empowered. You are not a victim of your decisions. Do not buy into the lie that you are powerless. That core belief will lead to self-sabotaging behaviors and will keep you from making optimal decisions. Decisions are made by you. Being a decision maker empowers you to make *new* decisions.

Honor your good intentions. Yes, you meant to watch your daughter's soccer game on time. That was the intention. Did you achieve it? No. Is that okay? No. Can you do better next time? Yes. Take the time to know your heart was in the right place. You were not maliciously trying to hurt your daughter's feelings by missing the game. The intention was to communicate your support and love. Intentions are desires based on your values. When you reevaluate the situation, identify the competing commitment and make needed adjustments. That may mean setting an alarm earlier, taking the work home, delegating the task, or any number of things to attend your daughter's game. If you believe there is no way to do it, think again. You did not get this far in life because solutions were simply handed to you. Make a way or adjust the expectations. People make mistakes because of misplaced priorities. Learn to show yourself grace and use that kindness to get better.

How do you properly recover from a bad decision? Recommit. Choose to do better the next time. Make a plan to do better. Being a trustworthy and reliable person is my core value. I do my best to fulfill my promises. I do my best to follow through with my commitments, whether it is being on time, completing a project, or taking out the trash. Sometimes I forget. Other times, I may procrastinate because of a competing commitment. In the past, guilt would eat me up and I would cruelly criticize myself. I began questioning my own integrity and became cautious about making any promises. Why commit if I might look bad for not keeping it? To maintain my integrity, I began playing the small game and stopped making commitments. My close friend, Danny, noticed my shrinking commitments and asked, "What's going on?" I told him, "I don't want to make promises I cannot keep. So, I stopped making promises at all and kept my expectations low! That way I won't fail anyone." Danny asked me, "Why not make commitments with the intent to keep them? If you break a commitment, apologize and renegotiate the terms of the commitment." Recommitment is the key. Declaring your commitment gives you direction and drive. When we fall short, learn why the commitment did not happen and adjust accordingly. The new information helps us revise the commitment to be more realistic.

Recommitment builds trust by demonstrating loyalty in a relationship. It invites a discussion. It keeps us in partnership with people. It is choosing to do life together through the highs and lows. We are not expected to commit perfectly. Unexpected things happen. But things can often be resolved with less devastating consequences through ownership and recommitment. How? Raise your intention, go back to the Framework, and commit again. Have the confidence to make a new commitment and keep it. Seize as many do-overs as life allows you to take. Know that if things do not work out, never stop making new commitments.

Recently, I was driving to my office to meet with a new client at 10:00 a.m. I left early and figured there was enough time to get to work, set up my office, and be ready for my client. Wrong. A semi-truck messed up its wheels and crashed on the side of the freeway, blocking three lanes, and stopping the flow of traffic. I started feeling anxious and frustrated about the situation. A stream of thoughts went through my head: "What's the point of getting up early if I'm going to be late anyways? I'm going to leave a terrible impression on my client. It's not even my fault. When is this traffic going to clear up?" At some point, being late was inevitable. I took a deep breath and made the call to the client to let him know the situation. I shared the reality that I would be there late and apologized. Based on my GPS, I renegotiated the time and asked to meet 10 minutes later. The client graciously accepted the proposal and a new commitment was set.

Recommitment requires a sincere apology. Assuming you had good intentions behind your optimal decision, there is no need to apologize for your good intention! Do not apologize for things that you do not actually mean; that is disingenuous. Rather, apologize that your decision contributed to the distress of another person. That means apologizing for the way things turned out despite your good intentions. Acknowledge your own disappointment or frustration. You can say sorry that the person involved feels disappointed in you or the unintended outcome. Apologizing for missed expectations communicates your care for the individual and helps repair the relationship. It can help soothe the aftermath. Apologizing is a posture of humility, and it means owning your involvement in the undesired outcome despite your good intentions.

Moreover, always take some time to reevaluate the situation. Why did the outcome turn out poorly? Ask yourself, "Was there something I did not consider or know?" or "What got in the way of making the right decision?" In every mistake, there is wisdom to be gleaned. What is wisdom? Wisdom is having the knowledge and ability to do what is right. Thomas J. Watson, former CEO of IBM, defined wisdom as "the power to put our time and our knowledge to the proper use."[93] Even if you made the same mistake over and over again, there is a revelation that needs to be captured. It may be a hidden fear or competing commitment. This is an opportunity to learn more about yourself. By identifying the factors that led to the bad decisions, you can use that information to amend your next commitment. It may mean staying away from certain people or settings that trigger a poor response. Or discovering the commitment is not what you really want. With the new information factored into the Framework, you are renewed with an updated mindset to make the next optimal decision.

Apply the wisdom you acquired and redeem your mistakes. We feel differently about our mistakes when we utilize our learnings to make a better decision in the future. Personal experiences can teach us what *not* to do and what to do. I remember going to Mexico and being sold a timeshare. The whole experience felt surreal and it seemed like the "right" decision until I got home. Although it was an expensive lesson, I am much more cautious with salesmen. I got a better deal on a new car by slowing down, leaving the dealership with my wife to discuss the deal, and purchasing the car a few hours later.

---

93   Quotable Quote. (n.d.). https://www.goodreads.com/
     quotes/53111-wisdom-is-the-power-to-put-our-time-and-our

Wisdom can also be acquired from people's mistakes. If you ask me, I would much rather learn from the wisdom of others! We do not have enough lifetimes to make all the mistakes ourselves. It is better to *be* humble and listen to sound advice than *being* humbled through "swallowing the bitter pill" of harsh experiences. Better to acknowledge one's folly now than to suffer through the mistake later! We can also gain wisdom from respected people who we do not personally know, through their books, movies, and audio recordings. Solidify your wisdom by integrating personal experiences with the wisdom of others.

Dare to make a new commitment. Start over with the Framework. Get clear on your intention based on your values and do things differently. The key word is "differently!" Since the last decision did not work, why would you do it the exact same way? That would be stupid! Unless you want to see the same bad thing happen again, something has to change. Work on thoughtful modification and communicating what you will do differently based on what you learned. This may mean leaving 15 minutes earlier for a meeting. Or improving your communication with your teammates by checking in with them before making a final decision. Dare to try something new, and that very thing may tip the scale in your favor and change your destiny.

CONCLUSION

Remember, a hero has the power of redemption. You are never too far gone. There is always a decision to be made. The choice to make a new decision based on your values is always yours to make. Learning from mistakes and doing better the next time is your redemption. It allows you to right your wrongs. Unconsciously, you can transform your past mistakes when you create a desirable outcome by applying what you learned. The meaning around the mistake gets shifted from "doing something stupid" to "gaining wisdom that achieved this victory." It fundamentally changes your past mistakes on a deep level; your narrative gets converted from senseless pain to redemption. How do you change the experience with your past? Create a corrective emotional experience in the present that rewrites your future self. Make a new decision that changes the negative association into a good one. Your brain interprets the past mistakes as a necessary progression to leverage that mistake into a win. The consistent shift over time increases your self-confidence as an optimal decision maker.

Ownership and Self-Trust

"I finally feel like me!" Meet Mary...again. "The divorce was really painful and I didn't see the light at the end of the tunnel. I had so much fear about the future. I worried about my kids and wondered what life would be like after the divorce. I didn't realize how much of myself was lost when I stopped advocating for myself. That reality finally sunk in with the separation and divorce. It took some time to get reacquainted with myself, but I'm thankful for the support of my family and church community. Through counseling, I continued to work through past pain and learned to love myself. I began making decisions that were aligned with my values, and something inside of me came back to life! There were definitely difficult days when I felt like giving up. After all, life stressors never gave me a break! Then I would remind myself of who I am and where I am going. I am putting my own voice and self-care as a top priority, and it made a huge difference. It is so refreshing to laugh and have fun again! I feel more myself than I ever have before."

Although the initial steps were not easy, Mary was able to identify what needed to be done, honored herself, and followed through with her optimal decision.

Joe, Mary's ex-husband, also turned his life around. When the divorce finalized, the consequences of his poor decisions finally hit him. "I will admit that it took me some time to get my life back together. I drank even more heavily and hit rock bottom before things became clearer. I owned my impulsive and selfish nature but was no longer going to accept that reality. One of the best decisions of my life was giving Alcoholics Anonymous a try, because I did not have the strength do it on my own. I met my sponsor, Doug, who understood my plight and patiently worked through the Framework with me. I realized that my marriage was over, but my chance to be a good dad was not. I have not drunk alcohol to cope in over five years, I hold a stable job, and I spend quality time with my kids every week. Both Mary and my family members share how much I have changed and seem so much happier. They are right! I became the better Joe I never knew existed. Through my experience, I know that it is never too late to be a better person."

Name the person that you admire the most. Who is it? Why do you admire them? I bet your person demonstrates the values you hold in a consistent manner. It is someone you would love to emulate and be more like. You may not like every aspect about this person, but the core parts of who they are stand out to you. I can guess that they make pretty good decisions. I'm not talking about never making a mistake. In fact, many of our heroes have made some major mistakes. They are our heroes because they turned things around by making better decisions that defined them in a positive way. So, how do you become more like the person you admire? By becoming an optimal decision maker.

Using the Framework will support you in becoming a person who takes ownership of his or her life. The Framework process has the power to fundamentally change and enhance who you are. The person you are today is the accumulation of all the decisions you've made in your life. Think about it. Every decision you made from brushing your teeth to getting married has defined the way you think and experience this life.

We are constantly being reformatted, molded, and changed depending on the decisions we make. Our personhood is much more than our thoughts because thoughts alone are still in the "imaginary" stage and unrealized. It is our actionable decisions that make those thoughts "real," and our feelings inform those experiences.

If you like the version of yourself right now, congratulations! You probably took the time to know and form your identity. Also, the majority of your decisions were executed in a value-affirming way. You have a general sense of control over your thoughts and actions. When difficult feelings arise, you are able to allow yourself to feel those feelings and understand the source of the emotions. There is a sense of fulfillment knowing how you navigated past pain and hardship with success. With those experiences, there is a genuine self-confidence and hopefulness for the future. There is an inner peace that rests in your authenticity and the ability to create desirable experiences.

If you are not satisfied with the version of yourself right now, then you are a work in progress! That simple acknowledgment allows you to stay in a growth mindset. To grow in loving yourself more, you must know yourself more. This is not just highlighting your weaknesses but it is also seeing yourself as a whole person. Identity formation is distinguishing your personal values and taking ownership of them. It requires sifting through the other voices and influences that may affect your self-identity to uncover your unique voice. We do not live in a vacuum, and therefore our identities are shaped through interfacing with people and situations. Through those experiences, there are parts of ourselves that stay fairly consistent. Those qualities contain the authentic version of yourself.

One of the reasons why self-love may be difficult is because of the comparison game. You may have bought into the lie that "successful" people need to look and act a certain way. If we don't look like what the media portrays as being successful or beautiful, then we are not enough. People are beautiful and powerful in their own ways. Is an apple more beautiful than a peach? Each fruit contains its own beauty, just like each person has his or her unique signature. The belief that satisfaction exists outside of your own personhood is the formula for unfulfillment. Even if satisfaction truly existed outside of yourself, what is the alternative choice? Pretending to be someone you are not. Many unhappy people refuse to accept their core selves, tormenting themselves with grievances and wasting resources to be somebody else. In the end, they are unhappy with their false self too! Learn to embrace those core parts of yourself that make you... you! Call yourself to a higher esteem.

What is self-esteem? To esteem something is to honor and perceive its value. By that definition, self-esteem is how a person perceives his or her own value. People with high self-esteem think of themselves as valuable and feel confident in their own worth. Those with low self-esteem perceive themselves with little to no value, which causes negative feelings. The interesting thing about self-esteem is that it is nothing more than a mindset. It is not tangible. You cannot touch or see self-esteem. It is largely arbitrary and subjective; a man-made idea to describe how a person perceives him or herself. So how do people determine their self-esteem? The concept is similar to love. You also cannot literally see or hold love. What you can see are the by-products of love. In the same way, people with healthy self-esteem carry themselves in a self-affirming and accurate way that helps them successfully navigate life's many challenges.

So how does someone increase their self-esteem? Become an optimal decision maker! The overarching purpose behind the Framework is to become an authentic person who is worthy of self-love. Making life-affirming decisions will define your identity and reveal your true values in different situations. The common values that arise from making good decisions will shape your optimal self. What kind of person are you? A person who makes good decisions. What kind of people make good decisions? People who are wise, self-aware, confident, reliable, and many other positive attributes. Increasing the hit rate in positive decision-making will fundamentally shift your self-perception and self-esteem. The other crucial element is perseverance. The enemy of self-esteem is giving up on yourself. It sends the message that you are incompetent and weak. Make the choice to keep fighting through the struggle. When you experience discouragement, take a break and recuperate. Understand the mistake and try again. Never give up on personal growth! Experiencing the victories of optimal decisions is what creates organic self-esteem.

Becoming the person you appreciate and honor is a day-by-day process. Begin by making the commitment to becoming an optimal decision maker. Make that a part of your identity. Honor yourself by making decisions that are aligned with your values. Don't feel it yet? Commit to the belief. Don't really believe it? Continue making self-honoring decisions until you do. Will you do this perfectly? Nope. Will you still make mistakes? You bet. Will you evaluate what went wrong and choose to be honest with yourself? That is up to you. Never waste a mistake. Learn from your faults by identifying what is misaligned with your identity. Identify the competing commitments that present as urgent "needs" in exchange for your authenticity. Or take ownership that your decision is actually aligned with your identity despite unfavorable results. There is an ebb and flow process where some decisions are based on our current identity while other times our decisions will help update our identity. Your identity is a work in progress with ongoing refinement. The authentic version of myself in my teenage years is pretty different from the authentic version of myself now. My value in being a good husband and father were not applicable to my younger self! Although the season of my life has changed, there are still fundamental qualities that have endured throughout my life. It is my commitment to stay true to who I am while being open to further growth in who I will become. It is choosing to improve in my decision-making and having the courage to move in the right direction again.

My biggest recommendation is to start with small optimal decisions. It is the same concept as taking baby steps. We do not expect ourselves to ride a bicycle before walking. Perhaps you have a history of making poor decisions. The time to change that track record is now! Begin with a healthy decision that can be executed simply and quickly. This could be something as ordinary as eating breakfast or brushing your teeth.

Retired Navy Seal Commander William McRaven stated, "If you want to change the world, start by making your bed. Nothing can replace the strength and comfort of one's faith, but sometimes the simple act of making your bed can give the lift you need to start your day and provide you the satisfaction to end it right."[94] Choose something that you can do every day with a high degree of success.

Wendy Wood, psychologist and author of *Good Habits, Bad Habits*, shared a practical way of making healthy decisions more consistent. She explained behaviors as having less friction or more friction.[95] To increase healthy behaviors, set them up to be accomplished easier with less friction. For example, let's say you forget to take your daily medication. Instead of keeping the medicine bottle in the kitchen cabinet, which is largely out of sight, move the bottle onto your nightstand next to a bottle of water. The opposite is also true about bad habits. Increase the friction by making the unhealthy behavior more difficult to do by adding more steps in order to get to it.

These changes may appear small but they add up over time. Making good decisions consistently will fundamentally change the way you see yourself. Your brain has to make sense of your unswerving good decisions! The shift will be a deep-seated feeling of being an optimal decision maker. After all, why else are you consistently making good decisions? You may not feel a difference

---

94 Goalcast. (2017). *William H. McRaven: If you want to change the world, start off by making your bed.* https://www.goalcast. com/2017/08/17/william-h-mcraven/
95 Wood, W. (2019). *Good habits, bad habits: The science of making positive changes that stick.* Farrar, Straus and Giroux.

in the first few days. Your self-talk may minimize your efforts by saying, "Big deal. You made a good decision today but you'll probably mess up tomorrow." After a few weeks, your brain will begin concluding that perhaps you are someone who follows through with their decisions. The consistency in making value-affirming decisions will create momentum. It is the daily victories that establish your confidence in making optimal decisions.

So how do you become an optimal decision maker? You started as an individual who either had trouble making decisions or made poor decisions, which created painful outcomes. Poor decisions are the by-product of an inauthentic and misaligned life. As we have all experienced, there are devastating short-term and long-term consequences for poor decision-making. We use the Framework as a step-by-step guide to properly evaluate the conflict and goal. We sift through our decision-making process to identify the best way to fulfill our needs. Use the acronym E-SORT to put the Framework together.

1. Emotions: What Are Your Feelings Telling You? The emotion question directs your attention to an important issue. Emotions are often raw and unfiltered. It is listening to our emotional world and using that information to be more honest with ourselves.

2. **Self-Values: What Matters to Me?** The Values of Self question identifies areas of meaning. We use that information to discover our core values, which uniquely define what matters to us and shape our identity.

3. **Others' Values: What Matters to Those Involved?** The Values of Others question brings the desires of other people into consideration. We expand our values to acknowledge that other people have their own values and aim to create win-win scenarios.

4. **Reality Factors: What Are the Facts Involved?** The Reality question identifies the more permanent factors that affect the options available. We acknowledge the reality factors that form our context in which we operate to create practical solutions.

5. **Tough It Out:** Pick your best option and courageously carry it out!

Using the Framework helps clarify the problem so that the choices are relevant and optimal given the circumstance. We take the known or newly acquired information from other sources to develop the optimal decision. Resistance to acting on the optimal solution is normal and expected. We must muster the courage to follow through with that decision and navigate the outcomes when they occur.

Perfection is not the goal. Instead, we're aiming for making better decisions more often and consistently. The only condition is to learn, apply, and continue to use the Framework in life's many decisions. Over time, the Framework process will become your natural way of thinking. Being an optimal decision maker will assimilate into your identity. The authentic person you become is the highest reward, and optimal decision-making will help you get there! Start today and know that forming your authentic self now will allow you to enjoy the person you become for many years in the future.

If you have any questions or comments regarding this book, I would love your feedback! Please share your stories if this book has helped you in becoming a more optimal decision maker. If you are interested in individual or corporate coaching on the Framework, consider working with me! You can reach me at *www.timyen.com*, email at *timkyen@gmail.com*, or Instagram at *@choosebetterconsulting*.

Acknowledgments

To the love of my life, Tiffany: You made this book possible in so many ways. When I think about being a better person, there is no one I want to be that for more than you. Your support through our discussions, encouraging words, caring for our family, creating space for me to create, and investing in our future mean more than mere words can express. In fact, many of the analogies in the book were birthed through our marriage! You do all these amazing things beautifully because you are a "natural." My relationship with you has made me a believer that I can courageously live out my values and experience deep love. Whatever I may contribute to this world, both now and in the future, let it be known that you created it with me.

To my son, Kairos: The world is an exciting place, and my wish is that you experience life to the fullest. Although I have my flaws, it is my highest honor to be your dad and someone who is privileged to guide your life. You will always make me a better person simply because you are in my life.

To my mother, Rita: Your presence and daily love for me has changed my life for the better. I thrived from the emotional safety you provided and feel my worth as a person because of your encouragement. I recognize how difficult life has been to come to America to give me these amazing opportunities. I push myself every day to live a life worthy of those sacrifices. Thank you for accepting me fully and believing in me.

To my father, Peter: I am grateful for your faithfulness to our family and your willingness to pursue your dreams. You inspire me to push the limits and believe for bigger things. You remind me that learning is a lifelong endeavor. When you say that you are proud of me, my heart grows a little fuller and bolder. Your values for God and His kingdom have profoundly impacted who I am.

To my other mother, Karen. On top of raising a wonderful daughter, you have been such a huge blessing to my life! Your selfless generosity has filled up my soul in such a deep way. Thank you for being a huge part of our family's life, and your concerns are much appreciated.

To my sister, Tiffany: You have been a huge encouragement and support ever since we were young kids. Your heart and compassion are bigger than your body can contain, which inspires me to be more selfless and giving. To my visionary brother, Danny Kang: Thank you for inspiring me to dream bigger and grow as a person. Introducing me to leadership development forever shifted the focus of my career. I look forward to what God will do through our lives and the impact we get the honor to make together.

To my closest friends: Howie Ju, Andrew Wu, Shaun Park, Kristina Park, Avery Kim, Ken Kim, Nicole Mesita, and Steven Mesita. Thank you for your steadfast loyalty as my confidants and supporters. You guys are my relational rock that gives me confidence knowing you always have my back.

To my fourth grade teacher, Mrs. Gaza: Thanks for seeing me as an "underchallenged" kid with potential instead of a troublemaker. It changed my narrative forever.

Special thanks to Epan Wu for giving me the initial idea to write a book on optimal decision-making!

To my mentors: James & Helen Yu, Eric Thaut, Rick Zuniga, Barry & Sunny Smith, Gabe & Cheri Barber, Marv Erisman, Larry Kuhn, Justin Choi, Jeff Hyun, Stephen Chong, Will Chen, Natasha Wen, Tim & Sheila Wu,

Samuel Lee, Josue Lee, Timothy H. Yen, Cathy Chang, Uncle John Koon, Cindy & Sol Levy, Mitch Keil, David Puder, and Derek Andrucko. Thanks for providing wise counsel and guidance in different seasons of my life. You saved me a lot of time and pain from figuring things out the hard way.

To the people who inspire me: Francis Chan, Ravi Zacharias, Brené Brown, Bill Johnson, Tim Ferris, Oprah Winfrey, Bill Gates, Brian Klemmer, Stephen Furtick, Stephen Curry, Jordan Peterson, Chris Chang, Dennis Kuo, Jeff Yen, Andrew Wai, and John Su. Your courage to live fully and the commitment to your craft have inspired me to know that anything is possible.

A huge thanks to all my past, present, and future clients. Thanks for the honor of hearing your story and doing the transformative work in counseling. I have learned so much through our work together, and it has shaped me in becoming a better psychologist.

And most importantly, all glory to God, the One who gives me my true identity and purpose.

About the Author

Dr. Timothy Yen is a psychologist with a strong passion to empower people to live their best lives. He received his Doctorate of Clinical Psychology with an emphasis in Family Psychology and consultation from Azusa Pacific University and certified in EMDR Therapy for trauma. Timothy has been counseling and supervising residents at Kaiser Permanente and his private practice for the past six years. Born in San Diego and raised in Orange County, California, with parents from Taiwan and Macau, he appreciates his bicultural heritage as an Asian American. He also served in the US Army as a mental health non-commissioned officer for over eight years. Timothy is an international speaker who teaches on topics such as leadership, faith, culture, and relationships in countries such as Taiwan, Hungary, and Kenya. He lives in the Northern California Bay Area with his wife, Tiffany, and their son, Kairos. Learn more about Timothy at *www.timyen.com*.

Made in the USA
Las Vegas, NV
24 October 2021

33025505R00148